PEARSON
REALITY CENTRAL
Real World Writing Journal

PEARSON

Upper Saddle River, New Jersey • Boston, Massachusetts
Chandler, Arizona • Glenview, Illinois • Shoreview, Minnesota

13-digit ISBN: 978-0-13-367513-9
10-digit ISBN: 0-13-367513-0

15 16 17   V011   17 16 15

TABLE OF CONTENTS

ABOUT YOUR BOOK

The What and Why of This Book

This book is designed to help you develop strategies you can use while learning about writing, grammar, usage, and vocabulary. While you write and work with vocabulary, you will return to the articles in your Student Anthology. You will think more deeply about the Big Questions.

Write About It!

Each article in your Student Anthology has an opportunity for you to Write About It! A writing assignment helps you think about the Big Question in a new way.

Draft It
A writing frame helps you organize your writing.

Writing Prompt
A prompt explains the assignment.

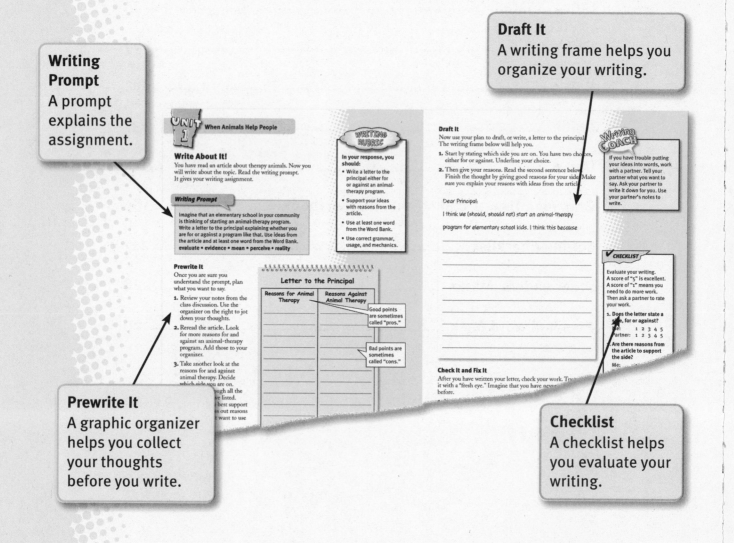

Prewrite It
A graphic organizer helps you collect your thoughts before you write.

Checklist
A checklist helps you evaluate your writing.

Vocabulary Workshop

Each article in your Student Anthology has a Vocabulary Workshop. In the workshop, you explore words from the Word Bank as you use them in different ways. Expanding your vocabulary will help you become a better reader and writer.

Your Choice
Record other words you want to remember.

Show You Know
Check your understanding about words by writing stories, crafting clues, or answering questions.

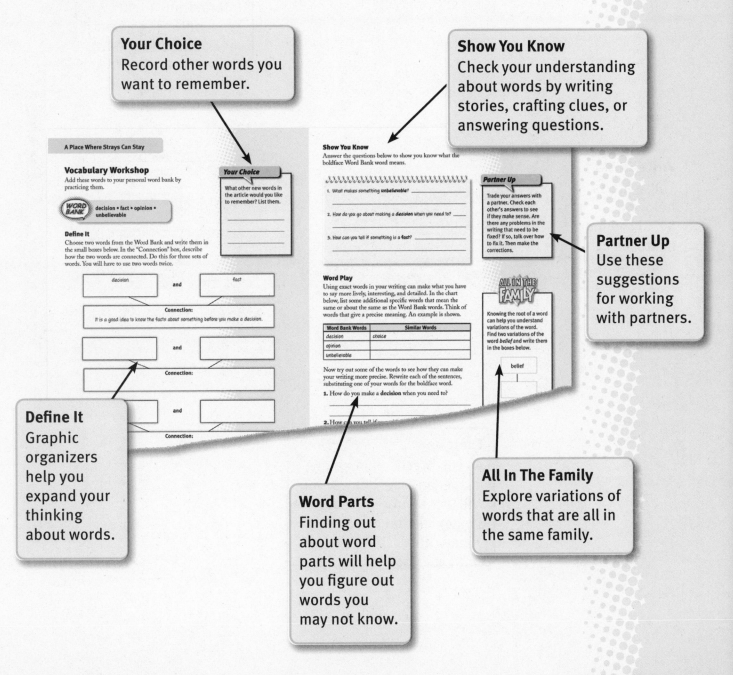

Define It
Graphic organizers help you expand your thinking about words.

Word Parts
Finding out about word parts will help you figure out words you may not know.

All In The Family
Explore variations of words that are all in the same family.

Partner Up
Use these suggestions for working with partners.

Grammar, Usage, and Mechanics Handbook

The Grammar, Usage, and Mechanics Handbook answers questions you may have during and after writing. It will help you correctly write and punctuate sentences. It will help you spell words that are commonly misspelled or confused.

Charts
Charts like this one help you find useful information about grammar, usage, and mechanics at a glance.

Writer's Alert
These alerts help you avoid common mistakes in your writing.

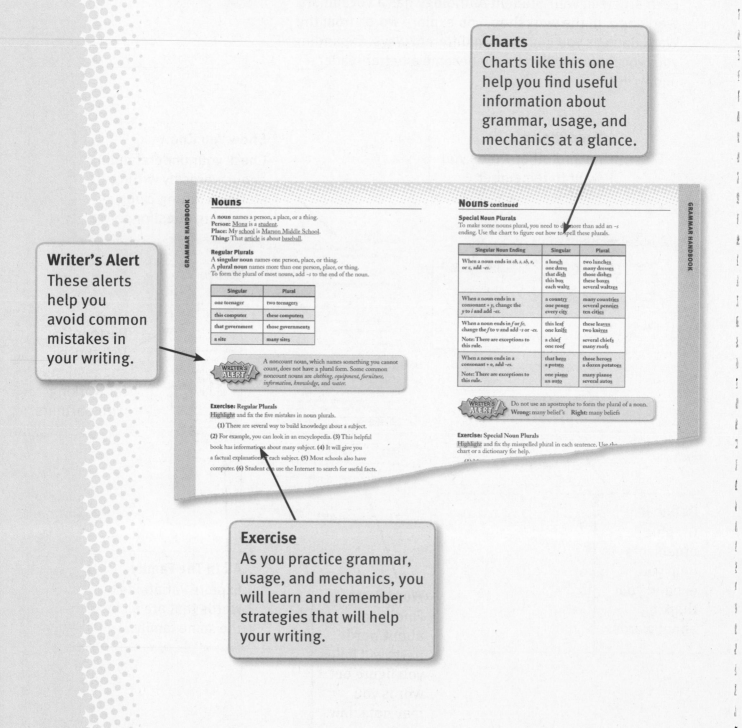

Exercise
As you practice grammar, usage, and mechanics, you will learn and remember strategies that will help your writing.

UNIT 1

What is the best way to find the truth?

Write About It!

You have read an article about therapy animals. Now you will write about the topic. Read the writing prompt. It gives your writing assignment.

Writing Prompt

Imagine that an elementary school in your community is thinking of starting an animal-therapy program. Write a letter to the principal explaining whether you are for or against a program like that. Use ideas from the article and at least one word from the Word Bank.

evaluate • evidence • mean • perceive • reality

WRITING RUBRIC

In your response, you should:

- Write a letter to the principal either for or against an animal-therapy program.

- Support your ideas with reasons from the article.

- Use at least one word from the Word Bank.

- Use correct grammar, usage, and mechanics.

Prewrite It

Once you are sure you understand the prompt, plan what you want to say.

1. Review your notes from the class discussion. Use the organizer on the right to jot down your thoughts.

2. Reread the article. Look for more reasons for and against an animal-therapy program. Add those to your organizer.

3. Take another look at the reasons for and against animal therapy. Decide which side you are on. Then read through all the reasons you have listed. Which reasons best support your side? Cross out reasons that you do not want to use in your letter.

Letter to the Principal

Reasons for Animal Therapy	Reasons Against Animal Therapy

Good points are sometimes called "pros."

Bad points are sometimes called "cons."

Draft It

Now use your plan to draft, or write, a letter to the principal. The writing frame below will help you.

1. Start by stating which side you are on. You have two choices, either for or against. Underline your choice.

2. Then give your reasons. Read the second sentence below. Finish the thought by giving good reasons for your side. Make sure you explain your reasons with ideas from the article.

Dear Principal:

I think we (should, should not) start an animal-therapy

program for elementary school kids. I think this because

_____

_____

_____

_____

_____

_____

_____

_____

_____

_____

Check It and Fix It

After you have written your letter, check your work. Try to read it with a "fresh eye." Imagine that you have never read the letter before.

1. Is everything written clearly and correctly? Use the checklist on the right to see.

2. Trade your work with a classmate. Talk over ways you both might improve your letters. Use the ideas to revise your work.

3. For help with grammar, usage, and mechanics, go to the Handbook on pages 189–226.

If you have trouble putting your ideas into words, work with a partner. Tell your partner what you want to say. Ask your partner to write it down for you. Use your partner's notes to write.

 **CHECKLIST**

Evaluate your writing. A score of "5" is excellent. A score of "1" means you need to do more work. Then ask a partner to rate your work.

1. Does the letter state a side, for or against?

Me:　　1　2　3　4　5
Partner:　1　2　3　4　5

2. Are there reasons from the article to support the side?

Me:　　1　2　3　4　5
Partner:　1　2　3　4　5

3. Is there at least one Word Bank word used?

Me:　　1　2　3　4　5
Partner:　1　2　3　4　5

4. Are grammar, usage, and mechanics correct?

Me:　　1　2　3　4　5
Partner:　1　2　3　4　5

Vocabulary Workshop

Add these words to your personal word bank by practicing them.

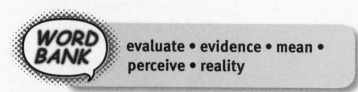

evaluate • evidence • mean • perceive • reality

Your Choice

What other new words in the article would you like to remember? List them.

_____

_____

_____

Define It

Complete the chart below by writing each of the words from the Word Bank. Write each Word Bank word in the chart. Then, tell what each word means. Finally, tell what each word does not mean. Use the example as a guide.

Word	What It Is	What It Is Not
evaluate	carefully decide how good or bad something is	say something is OK without looking at its good or bad points

Show You Know

To show that you understand the words, write three sentences. In each sentence, use and highlight two of the Word Bank words. You will use one word twice. Use the example as a model.

- What did the mysterious tire tracks and the other evidence mean?

1. _____
   _____
2. _____
   _____
3. _____
   _____

Partner Up

Trade sentences with a partner. Check each other's sentences. If something needs to be fixed, talk over how to fix it. Then make the corrections.

Word Endings: -ful, -ing

- A common word ending, or suffix, is -*ful*. This word ending means the same thing as the word *full*. When you add -*ful* to the end of a verb, you change the verb into an adjective.

  Verb: Guy and I **hope** you can play hoops with us today.
  Adjective: We are **hopeful** (full of hope) that you can come.

- Another common suffix is -*ing*. Adding -*ing* to a verb can change the verb into a noun.

  Verb: Maria and her sister **smile** when they are happy.
  Noun: Smiling makes Maria and her sister feel happy.

- Add -*ful* or -*ing* to the boldface word to make a new word that makes sense in the sentence. Write the word in the blank.

  My sister and I **read** every day. We love _____.

  I **hope** my little brother learns to read soon. I am

  _____ he will enjoy reading, too. Right now, he

  loves to **play**. He is such a _____ kid! My mom

  says _____ is a kid's job.

ALL IN THE FAMILY

These words from the article are part of the same word family. What are some other words that have the word *mean* in them? Add one to the list.

mean

meaningful

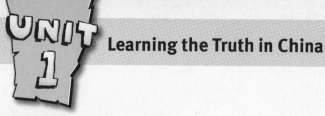

Write About It!

You have read an article about Internet censorship. Now you will write about the topic. Read the writing prompt. It gives your writing assignment.

Writing Prompt

After reading "Learning the Truth in China," how would you compare the Internet in the U.S. with the Internet in other countries? Write an informational article for the school newspaper explaining the similarities and differences. Use ideas from the article and at least one word from the Word Bank.

awareness • explain • factual • observe • reveal

WRITING RUBRIC

In your response, you should:

• Write an article for the school newspaper.

• Include similarities and differences based on the article you read.

• Use at least one word from the Word Bank.

• Use correct grammar, usage, and mechanics.

Prewrite It

Once you are sure you understand the prompt, plan what you want to say.

1. Review your notes from the class discussion. Use the organizer on the right to jot down your thoughts.

2. Reread the article. Look for ways the Internet in the United States compares to the Internet in other countries. Add similarities and differences to your organizer.

3. Do you need to change anything after rereading the article? Read through the similarities and differences on your organizer. Make needed changes, and underline the ideas you might use in your article.

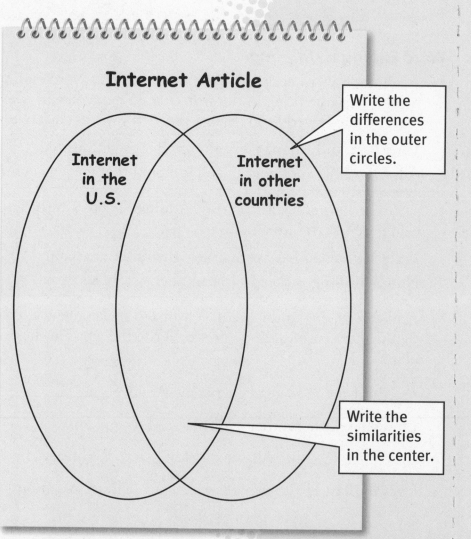

Internet Article

Internet in the U.S.

Internet in other countries

Write the differences in the outer circles.

Write the similarities in the center.

Draft It

Now use your plan to draft, or write, an informational article. The writing frame below will help you.

1. On the first blank line, write a headline, or title, for your article. Then read the first sentence in the frame. It states the main idea of your article.

2. Next, use the information from the organizer. Explain how the U.S. Internet is similar to the Internet in other countries. Then write about the differences.

Writing COACH

Newspaper reporters give facts, not opinions. In your article, describe differences without telling whether you think the differences are good or bad.

THIS JUST IN

My headline: _____

Did you know the Internet in the United States is similar

to yet different from the Internet in other countries? Some

similarities are _____

_____

_____

_____ .

Some differences include _____

_____

_____

_____ .

Check It and Fix It

After you have written your article, check your work. Imagine this is the first time you are reading your article.

1. Is everything written clearly and correctly? Use the checklist on the right to see.

2. Trade your work with a classmate. Talk over ways you could improve your articles. Use the ideas to revise your work.

3. For help with grammar, usage, and mechanics, go to the Handbook on pages 189–226.

✔ **CHECKLIST**

Evaluate your writing. A score of "5" is excellent. A score of "1" means you need to do more work. Then ask a partner to rate your work.

1. **Does the article state the similarities and differences clearly?**

   Me: 1 2 3 4 5
   Partner: 1 2 3 4 5

2. **Are there ideas from the text in the article?**

   Me: 1 2 3 4 5
   Partner: 1 2 3 4 5

3. **Is there at least one Word Bank word used?**

   Me: 1 2 3 4 5
   Partner: 1 2 3 4 5

4. **Are grammar, usage, and mechanics correct?**

   Me: 1 2 3 4 5
   Partner: 1 2 3 4 5

Vocabulary Workshop

Add these words to your personal word bank by practicing them.

 **WORD BANK** awareness • explain • factual • observe • reveal

Your Choice

What other new words in the article would you like to remember? List them.

_____

_____

_____

Define It

Complete the chart below. Write each Word Bank word, its meaning, and a word it reminds you of. Use the example as a guide.

What It Means	awareness	
knowing that something exists; having knowledge of something		**A Word It Reminds Me Of** realize
What It Means		
		A Word It Reminds Me Of _____
What It Means		
		A Word It Reminds Me Of _____
What It Means		
		A Word It Reminds Me Of _____
What It Means		
		A Word It Reminds Me Of _____

Show You Know

Write a comic strip in the space below using all of the Word Bank words in a way that shows you understand their meanings.

Word Endings: -*ness*

- When you add the suffix -*ness* to the end of an action word (a verb) you make a new word that is a noun.

  Verb: Kim is **aware** of everything that goes on in our school.
  Noun: His **awareness** makes him a great news reporter!

- Form new words by adding -*ness* to each of these words: *quick, sad, tough*. Then use the new words in the right places in the following paragraph.

  Kim is also a great football player. No one can run faster than he does, and that _____ makes him a good receiver. Moreover, his _____ enables him to get tackled without getting hurt. I will feel great _____ when he graduates this spring and leaves our middle school.

Learning the Truth in China

UNIT 1 — In the Grip of Graffiti

Write About It!

You have read an article about graffiti. Now you will write about the topic. Read the writing prompt. It gives your writing assignment.

Writing Prompt

Your town is thinking of setting aside a wall on a public building for graffiti artists to paint. Write a letter to the city council telling whether or not you support this idea. Use ideas from the article and at least one word from the Word Bank.

conclude • debate • evaluate • perceive • strategy

Prewrite It

Once you are sure you understand the prompt, plan what you want to say.

1. Review your notes from the class discussion. Use the organizer on the right to jot down your thoughts.

2. Reread the article. Look for more reasons that support or explain your opinion. Add those to your organizer.

3. Take another look at your opinion. Do you want to change it in any way after rereading the article? If so, make the changes. Read through all the reasons you have listed. Which are the best? Cross out the reasons that are not as good.

WRITING RUBRIC

In your response, you should:

- Write a letter to the city council giving your opinion on the idea of a graffiti wall.

- Give reasons for your opinion based on the article.

- Use at least one word from the Word Bank.

- Use correct grammar, usage, and mechanics.

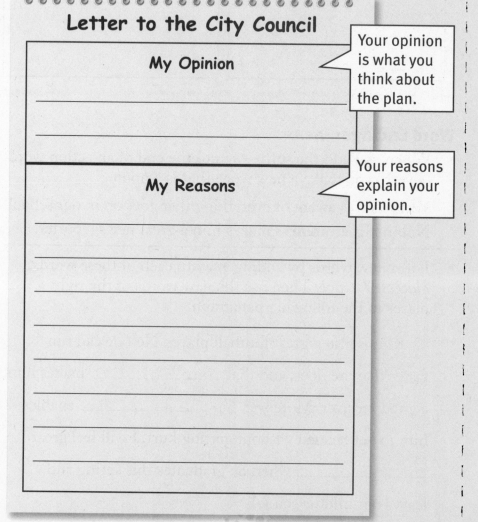

Letter to the City Council

My Opinion

Your opinion is what you think about the plan.

My Reasons

Your reasons explain your opinion.

Draft It

Now use your plan to draft, or write, a letter of opinion. The writing frame below will help you.

1. Start by giving your opinion. You have two choices of opinion. Underline your choice.

2. Then give your reasons. Read the second sentence below. Finish the thought by giving good reasons for your opinion. Make sure you explain your reasons with ideas from the article.

End your letter with the right closing. *Sincerely yours,* is a good way to end a business letter such as a letter to a city council. Sign your name after the closing.

Dear City Council:

I think the city (should, should not) set aside a wall for

graffiti artists. I think this because _____

_____

_____

_____

_____

_____

_____

_____

_____

_____

Check It and Fix It

After you have written your letter, check your work. Put it aside for a few minutes if you can, so that you can look at it with a "fresh eye."

1. Have you stated your opinion clearly? Use the checklist on the right to see.

2. Trade your work with a classmate. Share ideas for improving your letters. Use the ideas to revise your work.

3. For help with grammar, usage, and mechanics, go to the Handbook on pages 189–226.

✔ **CHECKLIST**

Evaluate your writing. A score of "5" is excellent. A score of "1" means you need to do more work. Then ask a partner to rate your work.

1. **Does the letter state an opinion clearly?**

   Me: 1 2 3 4 5
   Partner: 1 2 3 4 5

2. **Are there ideas from the article that explain the opinion?**

   Me: 1 2 3 4 5
   Partner: 1 2 3 4 5

3. **Is there at least one Word Bank word used?**

   Me: 1 2 3 4 5
   Partner: 1 2 3 4 5

4. **Are grammar, usage, and mechanics correct?**

   Me: 1 2 3 4 5
   Partner: 1 2 3 4 5

Vocabulary Workshop

Add these words to your personal word bank by practicing them.

 **WORD BANK** conclude • debate • evaluate • perceive • strategy

Define It

Complete the chart below. Write each Word Bank word in the first column. In the second column, write your real-life meaning for the word. In the third column, write your connection to the word. Use the example as a guide.

Word	Real-Life Meaning	My Connection
conclude	I try to get all the facts about a situation before I conclude what action I will take.	I conclude when my mom has started cooking dinner by the delicious smells.

Your Choice

What other new words in the article would you like to remember? List them.

_____

_____

_____

Word COACH

To remember new words, make connections with old ones. For example, it might be easier to remember *perceive* if you connect it in your mind with a more familiar word that means about the same thing, like *notice*.

Show You Know

In the space below, write a short, short story (just a paragraph!). In your story, use all the Word Bank words. Be sure your sentences show that you understand the meanings of the words.

Once upon a time, there was _____

_____

_____

_____

_____

Word Endings: *-able*

- As you might guess, the word ending *-able* means "able to." When you add *-able* to a noun or a verb, you change the word into an adjective.

  Verb: I tried to **debate** my new curfew with my parents.
  Adjective: They said their decision was not **debatable.**

- Add the suffix *-able* to each boldface word to make an adjective and complete each sentence.

1. enjoy (verb)

We had an _____ time at the party.

2. comfort (verb)

These well-worn jeans are my most _____ pair.

3. break (verb)

Be careful when you carry that _____ glass vase.

These words from the article are part of the same word family. What are some other words that have the word *debate* in them? Add one to the list.

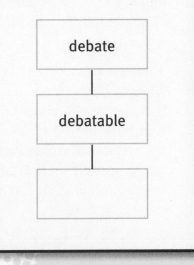

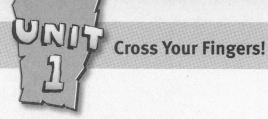

Write About It!

You have read an article about superstitions. Now you will write about the topic. Read the writing prompt. It gives your writing assignment.

In your response, you should:

- Briefly describe a superstition.

- Write a step-by-step experiment to test the superstition.

- Use at least one word from the Word Bank.

- Use correct grammar, usage, and mechanics.

Writing Prompt

After reading "Cross Your Fingers!" do you think superstitions can actually bring good or bad luck? Make up an experiment that could show a superstition is true or untrue. Write a step-by-step plan for your experiment. Use ideas from the article and at least one word from the Word Bank.

believable • explain • factual • fiction • view

Prewrite It

Once you are sure you understand the prompt, plan what you want to say.

1. Review your notes from the class discussion.

2. Reread the article. Look for a superstition you could prove or disprove, or use one you already know. On your organizer, briefly describe what the superstition is.

3. Take another look at your choice. Then think of a way to test whether the superstition is true. Write the steps of the experiment in the second section of the organizer. You can add steps if you wish.

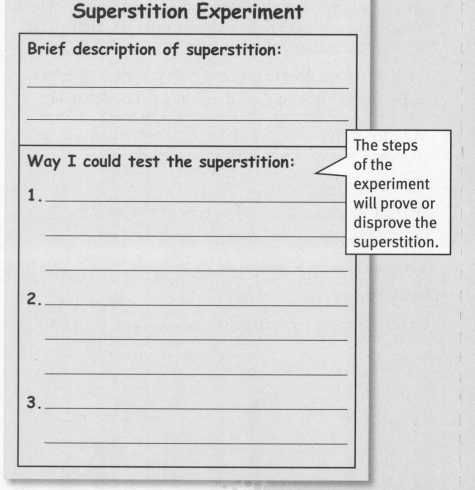

Superstition Experiment

Brief description of superstition:

_____

_____

Way I could test the superstition:

1. _____

_____

_____

2. _____

_____

_____

3. _____

_____

The steps of the experiment will prove or disprove the superstition.

Draft It

Now use your plan to draft, or write, the steps in an experiment. The writing frame below will help you.

1. Start by stating whether you will prove or disprove the superstition. You have two choices. Underline your choice.

2. Then describe the superstition your experiment will test.

3. Number and explain each step in the experiment.

To write about the experiment, picture how you would do the experiment. What would you do first? What would you do second? What would you do after that? These are the steps in your experiment.

The following experiment could be used to (prove, disprove)

a superstition. The superstition I will test is _____

_____

_____ .

The steps in my experiment are as follows. First, _____

_____

_____

_____

_____

_____

_____

_____

_____ .

Check It and Fix It

After you have written your experiment, check your work. Ask yourself these questions:

1. Is everything written clearly and correctly? Use the checklist on the right to see.

2. Trade your work with a classmate. Talk over ways you both might improve your experiments. Use the ideas to revise your work.

3. For help with grammar, usage, and mechanics, go to the Handbook on pages 189–226.

✔ **CHECKLIST**

Evaluate your writing. A score of "5" is excellent. A score of "1" means you need to do more work. Then ask a partner to rate your work.

1. **Is the superstition clearly described?**

   Me: 1 2 3 4 5
   Partner: 1 2 3 4 5

2. **Is each step in the experiment clear and sensible?**

   Me: 1 2 3 4 5
   Partner: 1 2 3 4 5

3. **Is there at least one Word Bank word used?**

   Me: 1 2 3 4 5
   Partner: 1 2 3 4 5

4. **Are grammar, usage, and mechanics correct?**

   Me: 1 2 3 4 5
   Partner: 1 2 3 4 5

Vocabulary Workshop

Add these words to your personal word bank by practicing them.

WORD BANK believable • explain • factual • fiction • view

Your Choice

What other new words in the article would you like to remember? List them.

_____

_____

_____

Define It

Choose two words from the Word Bank that could be connected. Explain their connection. Write the first word on the left side. Write the second word on the right side. Write the connection under the words. Repeat with the rest of the Word Bank words. One word will be used twice.

factual   **is connected to**   fiction

because: They are opposites. Something that is factual is real. Something that is fiction is made up.

_____ **is connected to** _____

because: _____

_____ **is connected to** _____

because: _____

Show You Know

Answer the questions below to show you know the meaning of each Word Bank word.

1. In what class might you **explain** your **view** of something? Describe why. _____

_____

_____

2. Which would be more **believable**: a **factual** news report or one that is **fiction?** Explain why. _____

_____

_____

_____

Partner Up

Trade answers with a partner. Make sure your partner's answers make sense. If they do not, talk about how to improve them.

Word Beginnings: *un-*

- The word beginning, or prefix, *un-* means "not." When you add *un-* to the beginning of a word, you change its meaning.

Believable: something you are able to believe

Unbelievable: something you are not able to believe

- Add *un-* to each of these words from the article: *believable, lucky, healthy, natural.* Then use each word to fill in a blank correctly.

1. Eating only potato chips and French fries would be an _____ diet.

2. After our team lost four games in a row, we were feeling _____.

3. The oil spill caused the ocean to have an _____ color.

4. A crazy lie would probably be _____ to the people who heard it.

Write About It!

You have read an article about bullying. Now you will write about the topic. Read the writing prompt. It gives your writing assignment.

Writing Prompt

Imagine that you write an advice column for your school newspaper. A student has written to ask your advice about the best way to handle someone who has been bullying her. What advice would you give her? Use ideas from the article and at least one word from the Word Bank.

awareness • consequence • evidence • pattern • truth

WRITING RUBRIC

In your response, you should:

- Write a letter responding to a request for advice.

- Describe a strategy for dealing with a bully.

- Use at least one word from the Word Bank.

- Use correct grammar, usage, and mechanics.

Prewrite It

Once you are sure you understand the prompt, plan what you want to say.

1. Review your notes from the class discussion. Use the web on the right to jot down your thoughts.

2. Reread the article. Look for more ways to deal with bullying. Add those to your web. Add more ovals if you need to.

3. Reread all the strategies you listed. Which do you want to explain in detail in your letter? Underline it.

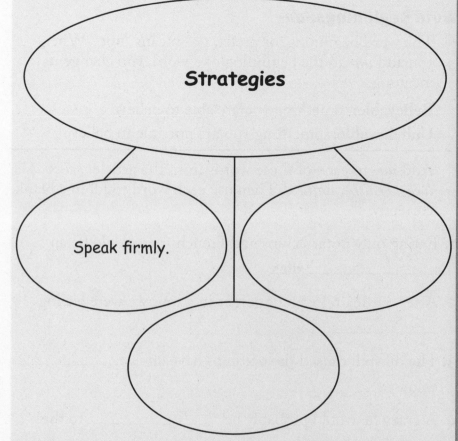

Strategies

Speak firmly.

Draft It

Now use your plan to draft, or write, a letter of advice.
The writing frame below will help you.

1. Read the first sentence. It gives the main idea of your letter.

2. Read the second sentence. Finish the thought by describing
the strategy you think the student should follow and why.

Dear Reader,

There are many good ways to deal with the problem of bullying.

I advise that you _____

_____

_____

_____

_____

_____

_____

_____

_____

_____

_____

Check It and Fix It

After you have written your letter, check your work. Try to read
it as if you have never seen it before.

1. Is everything written clearly and correctly? Use the checklist
on the right to see.

2. Trade your work with a classmate. Talk over ways you both
might improve your letters. Use the ideas to revise your work.

3. For help with grammar, usage, and mechanics, go to the
Handbook on pages 189–226.

Writing COACH

If you have trouble
describing the strategy,
imagine explaining it to
someone younger. How
would you say it? Have a
partner jot down your words.
Use them in your letter.

✔ *CHECKLIST*

Evaluate your writing.
A score of "5" is excellent.
A score of "1" means you
need to do more work.
Then ask a partner to rate
your work.

**1. Does the letter clearly
describe a strategy for
dealing with bullying?**

Me: 1 2 3 4 5
Partner: 1 2 3 4 5

**2. Does the letter use
ideas from the article to
explain the strategy?**

Me: 1 2 3 4 5
Partner: 1 2 3 4 5

**3. Is there at least one
Word Bank word used?**

Me: 1 2 3 4 5
Partner: 1 2 3 4 5

**4. Are grammar, usage, and
mechanics correct?**

Me: 1 2 3 4 5
Partner: 1 2 3 4 5

Vocabulary Workshop

Add these words to your personal word bank by practicing them.

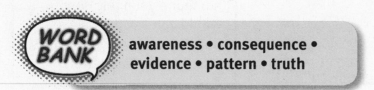

WORD BANK awareness • consequence • evidence • pattern • truth

Define It

Complete the chart below. First, tell what the Word Bank word means. Then tell what the word does not mean. Use the example as a guide.

Word	What It Is	What It Is Not
awareness	knowing that something exists	ignorance, having no idea that something exists

Your Choice

What other new words in the article would you like to remember? List them.

_____

_____

_____

Word COACH

You cannot remember new words if you are not sure how to say them. Use the pronunciation guides in a dictionary to figure out how to pronounce the words. If you need help, ask your teacher or a classmate.

Show You Know

Use the Word Bank words to write a dialogue, or conversation, between two people or characters. Make sure the dialogue shows that you understand each word's meaning.

_____ : _____
_____
_____ : _____
_____
_____ : _____
_____
_____ : _____
_____
_____ : _____
_____
_____ : _____
_____

It's Academic

All the words in the Word Bank are academic vocabulary. These are "school words" that you or your teachers might use in class. Choose three of the Word Bank words. For each word, write a sentence telling how you might use the word in one of your classes. Use the example as a model.

• In English, we learned that stories tend to follow a **pattern**.

1. _____

_____

2. _____

_____

3. _____

_____

 **UNIT 1**

Campers Give Peace a Chance

Write About It!

You have read an article about peace camps. Now you will write about the topic. Read the writing prompt. It gives your writing assignment.

Writing Prompt

After reading "Campers Give Peace a Chance," how would you describe peace camps to kids who were interested in going to one? Write a brochure for a peace camp. In your brochure, tell kids what the camp is like. Use ideas from the article and at least one word from the Word Bank.

convince • debate • fiction • insight • reveal

In your response, you should:

- Write a brochure describing a peace camp.

- Include specific details from the article.

- Use at least one word from the Word Bank.

- Use correct grammar, usage, and mechanics.

Prewrite It

Once you are sure you understand the prompt, plan what you want to say.

1. Review your notes from the class discussion. Use the organizer on the right to jot down your thoughts.

2. Reread the article. Look for more details about peace camps. Add these details to your organizer.

3. Reread all the details on your organizer. Decide which details would be best to include in your brochure. Underline them.

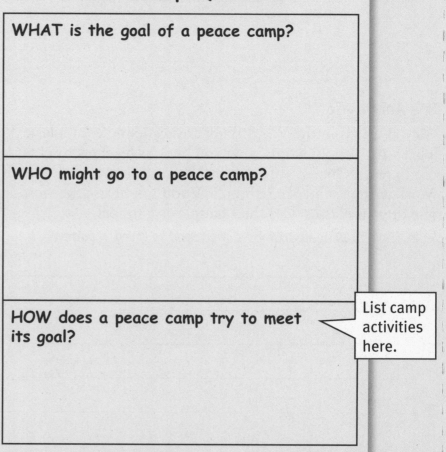

Peace Camp Questions

WHAT is the goal of a peace camp?

WHO might go to a peace camp?

HOW does a peace camp try to meet its goal?

List camp activities here.

Draft It

Now use your plan to draft, or write, a brochure. The writing frame below will help you.

1. Start by describing the purpose of peace camp. Tell what it is and who can attend.

2. Then give a description of the activities campers do at peace camp. Make the activities sound like fun!

Welcome to Peace Camp! Our camp is different from

other camps. The purpose of our camp is to _____

_____

Some of the kids who have attended peace camp

are from _____

_____

We have many great activities, including _____

_____

_____

_____

_____

Check It and Fix It

After you have written your brochure, check your work. As you read, imagine that you know nothing about peace camp. Does the brochure give you the information you need?

1. Is everything written clearly and correctly? Use the checklist on the right to see.

2. Trade your work with a classmate. Talk over ways you both might improve your brochures. Use the ideas to revise your work.

3. For help with grammar, usage, and mechanics, go to the Handbook on pages 189–226.

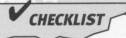

Writing COACH

If you have trouble putting your ideas into words, work with a partner. Read the ideas on your organizer to your partner. See what your partner understood from your ideas. This can help you to figure out where your writing needs to be clearer.

✔ **CHECKLIST**

Evaluate your writing. A score of "5" is excellent. A score of "1" means you need to do more work. Then ask a partner to rate your work.

1. **Does the brochure give information clearly?**

   Me: 1 2 3 4 5
   Partner: 1 2 3 4 5

2. **Are there details about peace camps from the article in the brochure?**

   Me: 1 2 3 4 5
   Partner: 1 2 3 4 5

3. **Is there at least one Word Bank word used?**

   Me: 1 2 3 4 5
   Partner: 1 2 3 4 5

4. **Are grammar, usage, and mechanics correct?**

   Me: 1 2 3 4 5
   Partner: 1 2 3 4 5

Campers Give Peace a Chance **23**

Vocabulary Workshop

Add these words to your personal word bank by practicing them.

WORD BANK convince • debate • fiction • insight • reveal

What other new words in the article would you like to remember? List them.

_____

_____

_____

Define It

Choose two words from the Word Bank to connect. Write the first word in the left box. Write the second word in the box on the right. In the center, write a sentence using both words. Repeat the process with the remaining words in the Word Bank. One word will be used twice. Use the example as a model.

debate	**and**	insight

My Sentence:
Hearing the two sides debate the issue gave me insight into it.

	and	

My Sentence:

	and	

My Sentence:

Show You Know

To show that you understand the words, write a clue for three words in the Word Bank. Exchange clues with a partner. See whether your partner can identify the correct word for each clue. Use the example for the word *fiction* as a model.

- A person who enjoys reading short stories and novels likes this.

1. _____

_____

2. _____

_____

3. _____

_____

Word Endings: *-ation, -ion, -tion*

- The suffixes *-ation, -ion,* and *-tion* mean "state of." When you add one of these suffixes to the end of a verb, you change the verb from an action into a noun, or thing.

  Verb: I will **reveal** my secret in an e-mail.

  Noun: The **revelation** will surprise you!

- Read the sentences below. Add one of the noun suffixes to each boldface word to complete the second sentence. Finally, write a sentence of your own using a word that ends in *-ation, -ion,* or *-tion.*

1. I can **imagine** what the characters look like when I read.

Use your _____ to picture the characters.

2. I **communicate** with my friends by cell phone and e-mail.

There are many forms of _____ to choose from.

3. A map can **inform** you of the best route to travel.

Look up the travel _____ on the Internet.

4. Write your own sentence using a word ending in *-ation, -ion,* or *-tion.* _____

_____

These words from the article are part of the same word family. What are some other words that have the word *reveal* in them? Add one to the list.

reveal

revelation

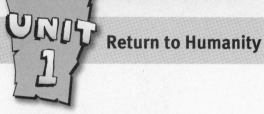

Return to Humanity

Write About It!

You have read an article about Ishmael Beah. Now you will write about the topic. Read the writing prompt. It gives your writing assignment.

Writing Prompt

Imagine that Ishmael Beah is coming to speak to students at your school. Write a speech introducing Beah to students at your school. Use ideas from the article and at least one word from the Word Bank.

affect • conclude • reality • truth

WRITING RUBRIC

In your response, you should:

- Write an introduction for Ishmael Beah that you could give at a school assembly.

- Give details about Beah based on the article you read.

- Use at least one word from the Word Bank.

- Use correct grammar, usage, and mechanics.

Prewrite It

Once you are sure you understand the prompt, plan what you want to say.

1. Review your notes from the class discussion. Use the organizer on the right to jot down your thoughts.

2. Reread the article. Look for more details about Beah and his life. Add those to your organizer.

3. Reread all the details you have listed. Decide which are the most important and underline them. Include these details in your introduction.

Ishmael Beah

Facts About Beah and His Life

Your facts form a short biography, or life story.

Draft It

Now use your plan to draft, or write, an introduction for Beah. The writing frame below will help you.

1. Start by welcoming Beah to your school.

2. Then give details about Beah's life. Read the second sentence below. Finish the thought by giving the first detail. Continue the introduction with additional information from the article.

Today we welcome _____ to our school. This young

man comes from _____. His life story is very

interesting. _____

_____

_____

_____

_____

_____

_____

_____

Check It and Fix It

After you have written your introduction, check your work. As you read, imagine that you know nothing about Beah. Does your introduction tell listeners what they would need to know?

1. Is everything written clearly and correctly? Use the checklist on the right to see.

2. Trade your work with a classmate. Talk over ways you both might improve your introductions. Use the ideas to revise your work.

3. For help with grammar, usage, and mechanics, go to the Handbook on pages 189–226.

Writing COACH

Try to make your speech of introduction interesting. Include important details that will make students want to listen to what Beah has to say.

✔ **CHECKLIST**

Evaluate your writing. A score of "5" is excellent. A score of "1" means you need to do more work. Then ask a partner to rate your work.

1. **Does the introduction state details about Beah's life clearly?**

   Me: 1 2 3 4 5
   Partner: 1 2 3 4 5

2. **Are there ideas from the article in the introduction?**

   Me: 1 2 3 4 5
   Partner: 1 2 3 4 5

3. **Is there at least one Word Bank word used?**

   Me: 1 2 3 4 5
   Partner: 1 2 3 4 5

4. **Are grammar, usage, and mechanics correct?**

   Me: 1 2 3 4 5
   Partner: 1 2 3 4 5

Vocabulary Workshop

Add these words to your personal word bank by practicing them.

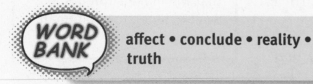

WORD BANK   affect • conclude • reality • truth

Define It

Complete the chart below. Write a Word Bank word in the first column. In the second column, write a synonym, or word that means the same thing. In the third column, write an antonym, or word that means the opposite. Use the example as a guide.

Word	Synonym	Antonym
affect	influence	ignore

Identifying synonyms and antonyms can help you remember what a new word means. Use a dictionary or a thesaurus if you cannot think of a synonym or antonym for a word.

Show You Know

In the space below, write a short, short story (just a paragraph!). In your story, use all the Word Bank words. Be sure your sentences show that you understand the meanings of the words.

Once upon a time, there was _____

_____

_____

_____

_____

_____

_____

_____

_____

Word Endings: -ive

- When you add the suffix -ive to a verb, you change the verb into an adjective.

  Verb: The members will **conclude** what they should do.
  Adjective: The results in their report are **conclusive.**

- The following words end with the suffix -ive: *competitive, imaginative, deceptive, effective, attractive.* Choose the correct word to fill in each blank.

1. I love to **imagine** what I will be when I grow up.

My mother calls me _____.

2. Jonah loves to **compete** on the basketball court.

He is _____ in school, too.

3. A dishonest person may **deceive** others.

It is hard to trust someone who is _____.

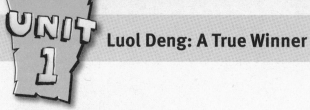

Write About It!

You have read an article about Luol Deng. Now you will write about the topic. Read the writing prompt. It gives your writing assignment.

Writing Prompt

Imagine you are helping Deng send mosquito nets to refugees. Write a note that can be included with each net. Explain what the net is for and who sent it. Use ideas from the article and at least one word from the Word Bank.

believable • convince • insight • rarely • report

WRITING RUBRIC

In your response, you should:

- Write a note that can be sent with a mosquito net.

- Explain what the net is for and who sent it.

- Use at least one word from the Word Bank.

- Use correct grammar, usage, and mechanics.

Prewrite It

Once you are sure you understand the prompt, plan what you want to say.

1. Review your notes from the class discussion. Use the organizer on the right to jot down your thoughts.

2. Reread the article. Look for more details about mosquito nets. Add those to your organizer.

3. Take another look at your organizer. Do you need to make any additions after rereading the article? If so, make the additions. Read through all the details you have listed. Which are the most important? Circle the details you will use in your note.

Mosquito Net

What It Is	How It Helps
Who Sent It	Why It Was Sent

Draft It

Now use your plan to draft, or write, a note. The writing frame below will help you.

1. Start by telling who sent the net.

2. Then describe what the net is, what it is for, and how to use it.

If you have trouble thinking of what to say, work with a partner. Have your partner read important parts of the article out loud. Together, put the parts in your own words. Use them in your note.

Dear Friend:

This mosquito net was sent to you by _____

_____.

The purpose of this net is _____

_____

_____

_____.

To use the net, _____

_____

_____

_____

_____.

✔ CHECKLIST

Evaluate your writing. A score of "5" is excellent. A score of "1" means you need to do more work. Then ask a partner to rate your work.

1. **Does the note tell who sent the net and why?**

   Me: 1 2 3 4 5
   Partner: 1 2 3 4 5

2. **Does the note clearly tell what the net is and how to use it?**

   Me: 1 2 3 4 5
   Partner: 1 2 3 4 5

3. **Is there at least one Word Bank word used?**

   Me: 1 2 3 4 5
   Partner: 1 2 3 4 5

4. **Are grammar, usage, and mechanics correct?**

   Me: 1 2 3 4 5
   Partner: 1 2 3 4 5

Check It and Fix It

After you have written your note, check your work. Try to read it with a "fresh eye." Imagine that you have never read the note before.

1. Is everything written clearly and correctly? Use the checklist on the right to see.

2. Trade your work with a classmate. Talk over ways you both might improve your notes. Use the ideas to revise your work.

3. For help with grammar, usage, and mechanics, go to the Handbook on pages 189–226.

Vocabulary Workshop

Add these words to your personal word bank by practicing them.

 believable • convince • insight • rarely • report

Your Choice

What other new words in the article would you like to remember? List them.

_____

_____

_____

Define It

Fill in the chart. In the center oval, write two or three subjects you could write about using the five words. In each box, write the meaning of a word from the Word Bank. Use the examples as a model.

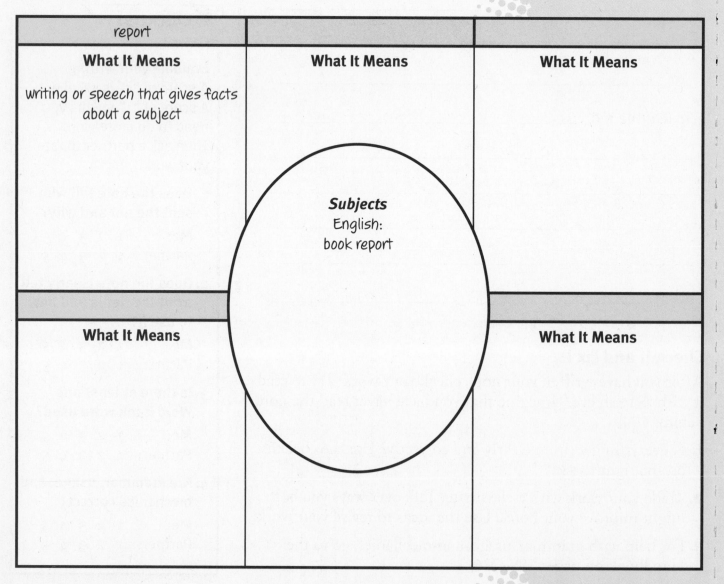

report		
What It Means	**What It Means**	**What It Means**
writing or speech that gives facts about a subject		

Subjects
English:
book report

What It Means | **What It Means**

Show You Know

Answer the questions to show you know the meaning of each
Word Bank word.

1. Is 245–81 a **believable** score in a soccer game? Explain.

   _____

   _____

2. Could you **convince** someone by giving reasons for an opinion? Why
   or why not?

   _____

   _____

3. Can a news **report** give you insight into a subject? Explain.

   _____

   _____

Partner Up

Share your answers with a
partner. Discuss whether
your answers are clear and
correct. Make changes if you
need to.

Word Endings: -edly

- When you add the suffix *-ed* to a verb, you sometimes
  change the verb into an adjective.

  Verb: Please **hurry** to the store.

  Adjective: Mario made a **hurried** trip to the store.

- When you add the word ending *-ly* to the new adjective,
  you change the word into an adverb.

  Adverb: Mario **hurriedly** went to the store.

- Read the sentences below. Add *-edly* to each boldface word
  and fill in the blank to make a new sentence.

1. "I will **repeat** the instructions," said the teacher.

   The teacher _____ explained the assignment.

2. Do you **suppose** our class will take a field trip this year?

   _____, we are going to a museum before graduation.

3. My cat is **content** to sit on the windowsill sleeping all day.

   The cat _____ licked her paws and cleaned her face.

These words from the article
are part of the same word
family. What are some other
words that have the word
report in them? Add one to
the list.

report

reported

reportedly

Writing Reflection

What is the best way to find the truth?

Look through your writing from this unit and choose the best piece.
Reflect on this piece of writing by completing each sentence below.

My best piece of writing from this unit is _____

_____

I chose this piece because _____

_____

_____

While I was writing, one goal I had was _____

_____

I accomplished this goal by _____

_____

_____

This writing helped me think more about the Big Question because

_____

_____

One thing I learned while writing that can help me in the future is

_____

_____

UNIT 2

Does every conflict have a winner?

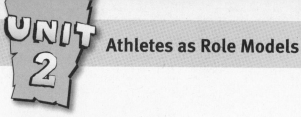

Write About It!

You have read an article about how athletes can act as role models. Now you will write about the topic. Read the writing prompt. It gives your writing assignment.

Writing Prompt

Imagine you are part of the World Sports Humanitarian Hall of Fame. Write a speech welcoming Dikembe Mutombo into the organization. In your speech, tell who he is and why he is a good role model. Use ideas from the article and at least one word from the Word Bank.
attitude • competition • disagreement • prepare • understanding

WRITING RUBRIC

In your response, you should:

• Write a speech to welcome Dikembe Mutombo to the hall of fame.

• Give reasons from the article of why he is a good role model.

• Use at least one word from the Word Bank.

• Use correct grammar, usage, and mechanics.

Prewrite It

Once you are sure you understand the prompt, plan what you want to say.

1. Review your notes from the class discussion. Use the web on the right to jot down your thoughts.

2. Reread the article. Look for the things Mutombo has done that make him worthy of the hall of fame. Add those to your web.

3. Take another look at your web. Do you need to change it in any way after rereading the article? If so, make the changes. Have you included details about Mutombo's accomplishments that show him to be a good role model?

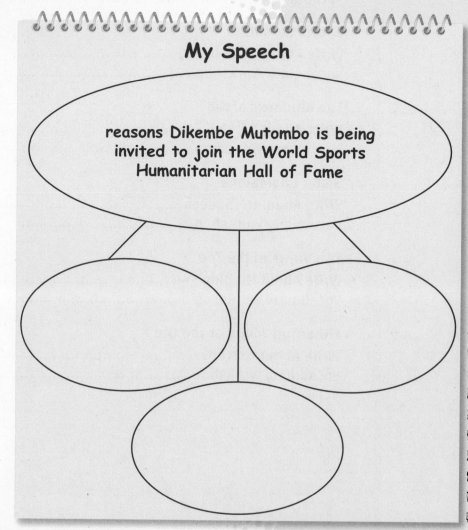

My Speech

reasons Dikembe Mutombo is being invited to join the World Sports Humanitarian Hall of Fame

Draft It

Now use your plan to draft, or write, a speech. The writing frame below will help you.

1. Start by explaining what the speech is about. Then give facts that support the decision to welcome Mutombo to the World Sports Humanitarian Hall of Fame.

2. Read the third sentence below. Finish the thought by giving strong reasons why Mutombo belongs in the hall of fame. Make sure you mention things about him from the article.

The World Sports Humanitarian Hall of Fame would like to welcome Dikembe Mutombo. He has done important things to help others. These things include: _____

_____

_____

_____

_____

_____

_____

_____

_____

Check It and Fix It

After you have written your speech, check your work. Try to read it with a "fresh eye." Imagine that you have never read the speech before.

1. Is everything written clearly and correctly? Use the checklist on the right to see.

2. Trade your work with a classmate. Talk over ways you both might improve your speeches. Use the ideas to revise your work.

3. For help with grammar, usage, and mechanics, go to the Handbook on pages 189–226.

If you have trouble putting your ideas into words, work with a partner. Tell your partner what you want to say. Ask the person to write it down for you. Use the person's note to write your speech.

Evaluate your writing. A score of "5" is excellent. A score of "1" means you need to do more work. Then ask a partner to rate your work.

1. **Does the speech tell how Mutombo has helped others?**

   Me: 1 2 3 4 5
   Partner: 1 2 3 4 5

2. **Are there examples from the article of what Mutombo has done?**

   Me: 1 2 3 4 5
   Partner: 1 2 3 4 5

3. **Is there at least one Word Bank word used?**

   Me: 1 2 3 4 5
   Partner: 1 2 3 4 5

4. **Are grammar, usage, and mechanics correct?**

   Me: 1 2 3 4 5
   Partner: 1 2 3 4 5

Vocabulary Workshop

Add these words to your personal word bank by practicing them.

 **WORD BANK** attitude • competition • disagreement • prepare • understanding

Your Choice

What other new words in the article would you like to remember? List them.

_____

_____

_____

Define It

Fill in the chart. In the boxes, write the meanings of the Word Bank words. In the center oval, write two or three subjects you could write about using the five Word Bank words. Use the examples as a model.

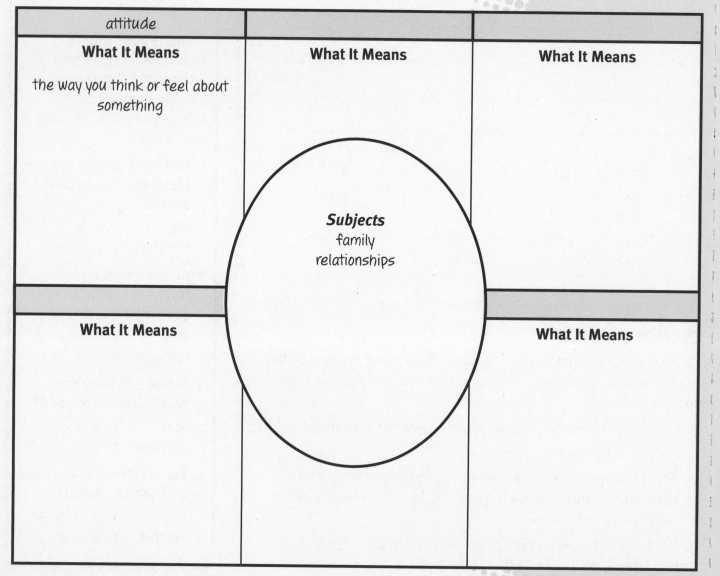

attitude

What It Means

the way you think or feel about something

What It Means

What It Means

Subjects
family
relationships

What It Means

What It Means

Show You Know

In the space below, write a short, short story (just a paragraph!) using the Word Bank words. Be sure your sentences show that you understand the meanings of the words.

Once upon a time, _____

_____

_____

_____

_____

_____

_____

_____

Word Beginnings: *dis-*

- When you add *dis-* to a word, you change its meaning.

  dis-: not, away from, apart

  _____

- Use the prefix to change the meanings of these words from the article.

  dis-: like, continue, honored

  _____

- Define each underlined word:

1. Incidents of cheating <u>dishonored</u> the entire school.

Definition: _____

2. Many fans <u>dislike</u> the attitudes of some professional athletes.

Definition: _____

3. His behavior will cause kids to <u>discontinue</u> admiring him.

Definition: _____

ALL IN THE FAMILY

Add suffixes to the word *agree* to create two other words in the same word family.

agree

Write About It!

You have read an article about coyotes living in cities. Now you will write about the topic. Read the writing prompt. It gives your writing assignment.

WRITING RUBRIC

In your response, you should:

- Write a letter to the editor to share your opinion.

- Give a reason for your opinion that is based on the article.

- Use at least one word from the Word Bank.

- Use correct grammar, usage, and mechanics.

Writing Prompt

Imagine that your community is planning on building a shopping mall where some coyotes live. Write a letter to the editor of your local paper and explain whether you are for or against building the mall. Use ideas from the article and at least one word from the Word Bank.

conflict • danger • outcome • struggle

Prewrite It

Once you are sure you understand the prompt, plan what you want to say.

1. Look at your notes from the class discussion. Use the organizer on the right to write down your thoughts.

2. Reread the article. Look for reasons that support or explain your opinion. Add these to your organizer.

3. Take another look at your organizer. Do you need to change it in any way after rereading the article? If so, make the changes. Read through all the reasons you have listed. Would they make readers agree with your opinion?

Letter to the Editor

My Opinion

_____

_____

Your opinion is what you think about a mall being built.

My Reasons

_____

_____

_____

_____

_____

_____

_____

_____

Your reasons explain your opinion.

Draft It

Now use your plan to draft, or write, a letter of opinion. The writing frame below will help you.

1. Start by giving your opinion. You have three choices of opinion. Underline your opinion.

2. Then give your reasons. Read the second sentence below. Finish the thought by giving a strong reason for your opinion. Make sure you explain your reasons with ideas from the article.

In a letter to the editor, you are trying to let readers know why they should agree with you. Choose reasons that will make sense to other people.

Dear Editor,

I think building a mall where coyotes are living is a(n) (great, OK, terrible) idea for our town. I think this because _____

_____
_____
_____
_____
_____
_____
_____
_____
_____

Check It and Fix It

After you have written your letter, check your work. Try to read it as if you are seeing it for the first time.

1. Is everything written clearly and correctly? Use the checklist on the right to see.

2. Read your letter to a classmate. Does your classmate agree with you? Use your classmate's responses to revise your work.

3. For help with grammar, usage, and mechanics, go to the Handbook on pages 189–226.

✔ CHECKLIST

Evaluate your writing. A score of "5" is excellent. A score of "1" means you need to do more work. Then ask a partner to rate your work.

1. **Does the letter give reasons for your opinion?**

   Me: 1 2 3 4 5
   Partner: 1 2 3 4 5

2. **Are there examples from the article that explain the opinion?**

   Me: 1 2 3 4 5
   Partner: 1 2 3 4 5

3. **Is there at least one Word Bank word used?**

   Me: 1 2 3 4 5
   Partner: 1 2 3 4 5

4. **Are grammar, usage, and mechanics correct?**

   Me: 1 2 3 4 5
   Partner: 1 2 3 4 5

Vocabulary Workshop

Add these words to your personal word bank by practicing them.

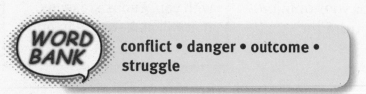

WORD BANK conflict • danger • outcome • struggle

Define It

Fill in the chart with the Word Bank words. Tell what each word means. Then circle the number that tells how well you understand each word. Circle "4" if you understand it completely. Circle "1" if you are not sure you understand the word at all. Use the example as a model.

What It Means	conflict
fighting between two sides who want different things	**How Well I Understand It** 1 2 ③ 4

What It Means	
	How Well I Understand It 1 2 3 4

What It Means	
	How Well I Understand It 1 2 3 4

What It Means	
	How Well I Understand It 1 2 3 4

Show You Know

To show that you understand the Word Bank words, write two sentences. In each sentence, use and highlight two of the words. Use the example as a model.

- There may be danger for people who live near where a conflict happens.

1. _____

   _____

2. _____

   _____

Partner Up

Trade sentences with a partner. Check each other's sentences. If something needs to be fixed, talk over how to fix it. Then make corrections.

Prefixes: *em-, en-*

- Prefixes can tell something about the words that follow. The prefixes *em-* and *en-* mean "cause to be." Using one of these prefixes means that the word that follows will "happen" or "be." What does the word *enable* mean in the following sentence? Find and think about the parts of the word.

  Practicing his instrument would **enable** Carlos to join the band.

- Look at each boldface word and write a definition.

1. State representatives voted to **enact** a new law.

   Definition: _____

2. Some tribes tried to **enslave** members of enemy tribes.

   Definition: _____

3. Citizens of a country **empower** themselves when they vote.

   Definition: _____

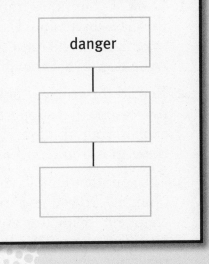

Find two other words in the article that are in the same word family as *danger*.

danger

Write About It!

You have read an article about parents who serve as soldiers in the military. Now you will write about the topic. Read the writing prompt. It gives your writing assignment.

Writing Prompt

Imagine that you are a reporter for a teen news radio show. You have been asked to do a broadcast. Write a script for yourself. A script is like a speech you memorize or read out loud. Tell your opinion on whether we need new laws to protect parents in the military. Use ideas from the article and at least one word from the Word Bank.

desire • opposition • plan • resolution

WRITING RUBRIC

In your response, you should:

- Write a script telling your opinion.

- Give a reason for your opinion that is based on the article.

- Use at least one word from the Word Bank.

- Use correct grammar, usage, and mechanics.

Prewrite It

Once you are sure you understand the prompt, plan what you want to say.

1. Look at your notes from the class discussion. Use the organizer on the right to write down your thoughts.

2. Reread the article. Look for reasons that support or explain your opinion. Add these to your organizer.

3. Take another look at your opinion. Do you need to change it in any way after rereading the article? If so, make the changes. Read through all the reasons you have listed. Which are the strongest? Cross out the reasons that are not as strong.

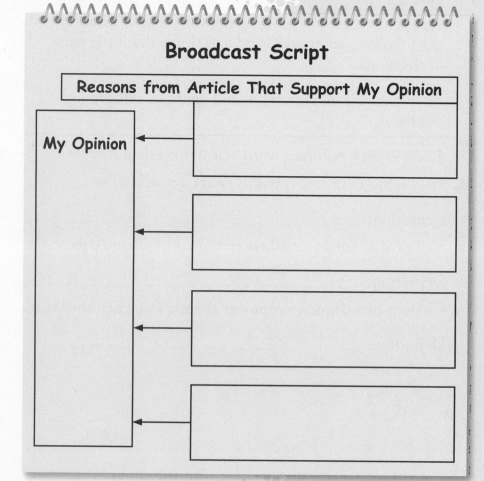

Broadcast Script

Reasons from Article That Support My Opinion

My Opinion

Draft It

Now use your plan to draft, or write, your broadcast script. The writing frame below will help you.

1. Give your opinion. You have two choices of opinion. Underline your choice.

2. Then give your reasons. Make sure you explain your reasons with ideas from the article.

Teen Radio News Broadcast

Radio Announcer: Today's topic is "Do we need new laws to protect parents in the military?" We (do, do not) need new laws. I think this because _____

_____

_____

_____

_____

_____

_____

_____

Check It and Fix It

After you have written your radio broadcast script, check your work. Read it out loud. Imagine you are hearing it on the radio.

1. Is everything written clearly and correctly? Use the checklist on the right to see.

2. Read your broadcast to a classmate. Ask your classmate if your reasons are convincing. Use your classmate's responses to revise your work.

3. For help with grammar, usage, and mechanics, go to the Handbook on pages 189–226.

✔ **CHECKLIST**

Evaluate your writing. A score of "5" is excellent. A score of "1" means you need to do more work. Then ask a partner to rate your work.

1. **Does the script give reasons that support the opinion?**

   Me: 1 2 3 4 5
   Partner: 1 2 3 4 5

2. **Are there examples from the article that explain the opinion?**

   Me: 1 2 3 4 5
   Partner: 1 2 3 4 5

3. **Is there at least one Word Bank word used?**

   Me: 1 2 3 4 5
   Partner: 1 2 3 4 5

4. **Are grammar, usage, and mechanics correct?**

   Me: 1 2 3 4 5
   Partner: 1 2 3 4 5

Vocabulary Workshop

Add these words to your personal word bank by practicing them.

 **WORD BANK** desire • opposition • plan • resolution

Define It

Complete the chart below. Write the Word Bank words in the chart. Then, tell what each word means. Finally, tell what each word does not mean. Use the example as a guide.

Word	What It Is	What It Is Not
desire	having a strong wish or need for something	not wanting something

Your Choice

What other new words in the article would you like to remember? List them.

_____

_____

_____

 **Word COACH**

The best way to remember new words is to use them. Pick a new word each week. Each day of that week, practice using the word while talking to your friends, teachers, and parents.

Show You Know

To show that you understand the Word Bank words, write a clue for each word. Exchange clues with a partner. See whether your partner can identify the correct word for each clue. Use the clue for the word *plan* as a model.

- If you are going to do something the right way, it helps to have this in place before you start.

1. _____

2. _____

3. _____

4. _____

Multiple-Meaning Words

- When you use a dictionary to find the meaning of a word, you often find more than one definition for the word. How can you tell which is the right one? Look at how the word is used in the context of a sentence. For example, which definition for *plan* makes sense below?

Hernan had a clear **plan** of how to help his sister.

plan: (a) a method of doing something; (b) to intend to do something

If you chose definition (a), you are right. That definition makes sense in the sentence.

- Circle the correct meaning for each boldface word in the chart below.

Word in Sentence	Meaning 1	Meaning 2
The teacher said they had to **face** the fact that studying was the only way to learn.	front of the head, which features the eyes, nose, and mouth	to accept something to be true
Marta could easily **picture** the warm days of summer.	a photograph	to imagine something
Olivia knew that growing up would be a **sum** of good and bad days.	the total amount of something	to add up a series of numbers

UNIT 2 Sports Parents

Write About It!

You have read an article about the behavior of some parents whose kids play competitive sports. Now you will write about the topic. Read the writing prompt. It gives your writing assignment.

Writing Prompt

Imagine that you are a coach for a recreation program for younger kids. Write a letter to tell parents how kids benefit from playing sports. Explain how parents can help kids have fun without pressuring them. Use ideas from the article and at least one word from the Word Bank.

communication • competition • compromise • misunderstanding • perform

Prewrite It

Once you are sure you understand the prompt, plan what you want to say.

1. Take another look at your notes from the class discussion. Use the organizer on the right to write down your thoughts.

2. Reread the article. Look for facts that support the benefits of kids' sports. Add these to your organizer.

3. Take another look at your organizer. Is there an important point you may have left out? If so, make a change. Read through all the points you have listed. Circle the strongest reasons and cross out the others.

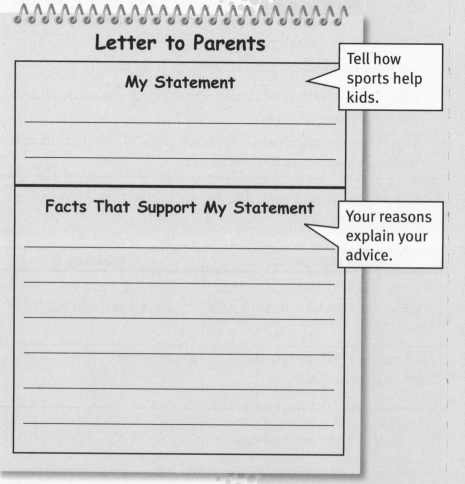

Letter to Parents

My Statement

Tell how sports help kids.

Facts That Support My Statement

Your reasons explain your advice.

Draft It

Now use your plan to draft, or write, a letter of advice. The writing frame below will help you.

1. Start by making your statement.

2. Then give facts from the article that support your statement. Read the second sentence below. Finish the statement by giving information from the article.

Dear Parents:

Your kids will enjoy our recreation group. You can help them

have fun when they compete in sports by _____

_____

_____

_____

_____

_____

_____

_____

_____

_____

_____

_____

If you have trouble putting ideas into words, look for examples in the article of what parents should *not* do. Write these down. Then write down what the opposite actions would be. These would be things parents *should* do to help the kids have fun.

✔ **CHECKLIST**

Evaluate your writing. A score of "5" is excellent. A score of "1" means you need to do more work. Then ask a partner to rate the work.

1. Does your letter give reasons to support the statement?

Me: 1 2 3 4 5
Partner: 1 2 3 4 5

2. Are there examples from the article that explain the statement?

Me: 1 2 3 4 5
Partner: 1 2 3 4 5

3. Is there at least one Word Bank word used?

Me: 1 2 3 4 5
Partner: 1 2 3 4 5

4. Are grammar, usage, and mechanics correct?

Me: 1 2 3 4 5
Partner: 1 2 3 4 5

Check It and Fix It

After you have written your letter, check your work. Read it as if you are a parent, looking for tips about your kids and sports.

1. Is everything written clearly and correctly? Use the checklist on the right to see.

2. Trade your work with a classmate. Talk over ways you might both improve your letters. Use the ideas to revise your work.

3. For help with grammar, usage, and mechanics, go to the Handbook on pages 189–226.

Vocabulary Workshop

Add these words to your personal word bank by practicing them.

communication • competition • compromise • misunderstanding • perform

Your Choice

What other new words in the article would you like to remember? List them.

_____

_____

_____

Define It

Complete the chart below. Write each Word Bank word in the first column. In the second column, write a real-life example of the word. In the third column, write your connection to the word. Use the example as a guide.

Word	Real-Life Example	My Connection to the Word
communication	Two forms of communication I use every day are text messaging and e-mail.	The best way for me to communicate is by text message.

Show You Know

Using all of the Word Bank words, write a dialogue between two characters. Make sure the dialogue shows that you understand the words' meanings.

_____ : _____
                  _____
_____ : _____
                  _____
_____ : _____
                  _____
_____ : _____
                  _____

Partner Up

Read one of the sentences in your dialogue out loud. Have your partner read another. Talk over whether the two sentences work together to show you know what the Word Bank words mean.

Word Beginnings: *mis-*

- The prefix *mis-* means "bad" or "wrong." When *mis-* is added in front of a word, it means that the action described in the word is being done wrongly.

- Write the meanings of the new words formed by adding *mis-*.

Prefix		Word		New Word	Meaning
mis	+	behave	=	misbehave	behave badly or wrongly
mis	+	trust	=	mistrust	
mis	+	fortune	=	misfortune	
mis	+	understand	=	misunderstand	

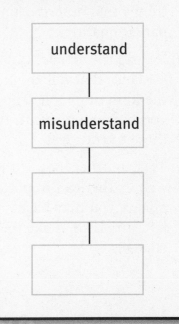

ALL IN THE FAMILY

The following words are in the same word family. What are some other words that have *understand* in them? Add two to the list.

| understand |

| misunderstand |

| |

| |

Write About It!

You have read an article about kinship parenting. Now you will write about the topic. Read the writing prompt. It gives your writing assignment.

In your response, you should:

- Write a list of kinship parent qualities.

- Support your list with information from the article.

- Use at least one word from the Word Bank.

- Use correct grammar, usage, and mechanics.

Writing Prompt

What kinds of qualities should kinship parents have? Make a list of qualities you think are most important for someone becoming a kinship parent. When you have completed your list, write whether you think being a kinship parent is worth the sacrifice. Try to use ideas from the article. Use at least one word from the Word Bank.

assume • challenge • desire • obstacle • understanding

Prewrite It

Once you are sure you understand the prompt, plan what you want to say.

1. Review your notes from the class discussion. Use the web on the right to write things that describe kinship parent qualities.

2. Reread the article. Look for clues that tell about the kind of people who are good kinship parents. Add these to your web.

3. Take another look at the web. Is there an important quality you may have left out? If so, make the changes.

Kinship Parent Qualities

Good Kinship Parents

Put qualities of good kinship parents in these circles.

Draft It

Now use your plan to draft, or write, your list of important kinship parent qualities. The writing frame below will help you.

1. Under the first sentence, list at least three qualities a person needs to be a good kinship parent. Finish the second sentence by underlining the word that gives your opinion.

2. Then give reasons for your opinion. Try to use ideas from the article.

If you have trouble putting ideas into words, work with a partner. Tell your partner what you want to say. Ask the partner to write it down. Use the person's notes to make your list and write.

Qualities

A kinship parent should be: _____

_____

_____

_____

_____

I think that being a kinship parent (is, is not) worth the

sacrifice. I think this because _____

_____

_____

_____

_____

✔ CHECKLIST

Evaluate your writing. A score of "5" is excellent. A score of "1" means you need to do more work. Then ask a partner to rate your work.

1. **Does the list give qualities of a good kinship parent?**

   Me: 1 2 3 4 5
   Partner: 1 2 3 4 5

2. **Are there ideas from the article used in the writing?**

   Me: 1 2 3 4 5
   Partner: 1 2 3 4 5

3. **Is there at least one Word Bank word?**

   Me: 1 2 3 4 5
   Partner: 1 2 3 4 5

4. **Are grammar, usage, and mechanics correct?**

   Me: 1 2 3 4 5
   Partner: 1 2 3 4 5

Check It and Fix It

After you have written your list, check your work. Try to look at it with a "fresh eye." If you knew nothing about kinship parents, would this list help you understand the topic?

1. Is everything written clearly and correctly? Use the checklist on the right to see.

2. Trade your work with a classmate. Talk over the reasons for your opinions. Use the ideas to revise your work.

3. For help with grammar, usage, and mechanics, go to the Handbook on pages 189–226.

Vocabulary Workshop

Add these words to your personal word bank by practicing them.

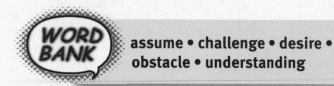

WORD BANK assume • challenge • desire • obstacle • understanding

Your Choice

What other new words in the article would you like to remember? List them.

_____

_____

_____

Define It

Use this chart to help you better understand the meanings of the Word Bank words. Follow the example to decide what each word means and what it does not mean.

Word	What It Is	What It Is Not
assume	thinking that something is true without making sure	knowing the facts before deciding something is true or not

Show You Know

In the space below, write a short, short story (just a paragraph!) using the Word Bank words. Be sure your sentences show that you understand the meanings of the words.

Once upon a time, _____

_____

_____

_____

_____

Word Play

Using exact words in your writing can make what you have to say more interesting and specific. In the chart below, list some more specific words that mean the same or about the same as the Word Bank words.

Word Bank Words	Similar Words
obstacle	hurdle, blockage, barrier
desire	wish, craving, eagerness

Now try out some of the words to see how they can make your writing more specific. Rewrite each of the sentences below. Substitute one of your words for the boldface word.

1. Karen's shyness is an **obstacle** to making the debate team.

_____

2. Playing soccer all day increased Peter's **desire** for a cool drink.

_____

UNIT 2 · Sister Champions

Write About It!

You have read an article about how Venus and Serena Williams handle competition in professional tennis. Now you will write about the topic. Read the writing prompt. It gives your writing assignment.

Writing Prompt

Imagine that you have been asked to do a presentation on competition at a neighborhood elementary school. Write a short speech to share your opinion on lessons kids can learn from Venus and Serena Williams. Use ideas from the article and at least one word from the Word Bank.

attitude • conflict • obstacle • opposition • style

Prewrite It

Once you are sure you understand the prompt, plan what you want to say.

1. Which notes from the class discussion can you use to support your opinion? Use the organizer on the right to jot down your thoughts.

2. Reread the article. Look for additional reasons that explain your opinion. Add these to your organizer.

3. Take another look at your opinion. Do you need to change it in any way after rereading the article? If so, make the changes.

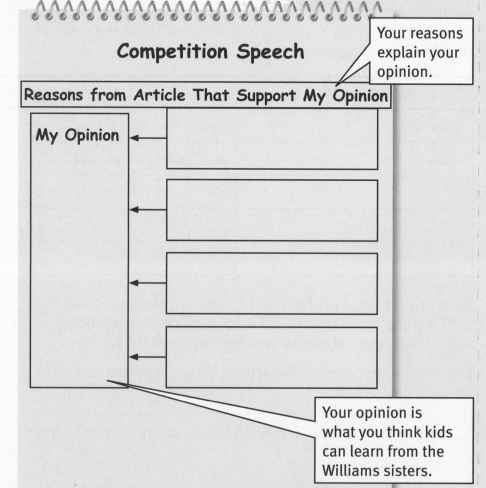

Competition Speech

Your reasons explain your opinion.

Reasons from Article That Support My Opinion

My Opinion

Your opinion is what you think kids can learn from the Williams sisters.

Draft It

Now use your plan to draft, or write, your speech. The writing frame below will help you.

1. Start by giving your opinion. Underline one of the available choices.

2. Then give your reasons. Read the second sentence below. Finish the thought by giving a strong reason for your opinion. Explain your reason with ideas from the article.

Writing COACH

When writing a speech, it helps to make an outline of the main points of the speech. Use the outline to remind yourself of what you want to say and the order in which you want to say it.

Presentation Speech

Kids can learn (very important/somewhat important/not very important) lessons from Serena and Venus Williams. I think this because _____

_____

_____

_____

_____

_____

_____

_____

_____

_____

_____

✔ CHECKLIST

Evaluate your writing. A score of "5" is excellent. A score of "1" means you need to do more work. Then ask a partner to rate your work.

1. **Does the speech state the opinion clearly?**

   Me: 1 2 3 4 5
   Partner: 1 2 3 4 5

2. **Are there ideas from the article that explain the opinion?**

   Me: 1 2 3 4 5
   Partner: 1 2 3 4 5

3. **Is there at least one Word Bank word used?**

   Me: 1 2 3 4 5
   Partner: 1 2 3 4 5

4. **Are grammar, usage, and mechanics correct?**

   Me: 1 2 3 4 5
   Partner: 1 2 3 4 5

Check It and Fix It

After you have written your speech, check your work.

1. Is everything written clearly and correctly? Use the checklist on the right to see.

2. Read your speech out loud to a classmate. Talk over the reasons for your opinions. Use the ideas to revise your work.

3. For help with grammar, usage, and mechanics, go to the Handbook on pages 189–226.

Vocabulary Workshop

Add these words to your personal word bank by practicing them.

 **WORD BANK** attitude • conflict • obstacle • opposition • style

Your Choice

What other new words in the article would you like to remember? List them.

_____

_____

_____

Define It

Complete the chart below. Write each Word Bank word, its meaning, and a word it reminds you of. Use the example as a guide.

What It Means	style
a particular way of doing something	**A Word It Reminds Me Of** method
What It Means	
	A Word It Reminds Me Of _____
What It Means	
	A Word It Reminds Me Of _____
What It Means	
	A Word It Reminds Me Of _____
What It Means	
	A Word It Reminds Me Of _____

Show You Know

Write a comic strip in the space below using all of the Word Bank words. Make sure the comic strip shows that you understand the words' meanings.

Partner Up

Trade comic strips with a partner. Read through each other's comic strips silently, and then read each aloud. Revise any language that is unclear.

Root Words

- Words are often built on core, or root, words. Knowing what the root means can help you figure out the meaning of new words.

- Root words are sometimes based on Greek or Latin. For example, the root *pos* or *posit* is taken from a Latin word meaning "to place or to put." Often, root words are combined with prefixes or suffixes to form new words.

- Try to figure out the meaning of each word in the table below. Look at the meaning of the prefix, and add it to the meaning of the root. Write the definition of the new word in the Word Meaning column.

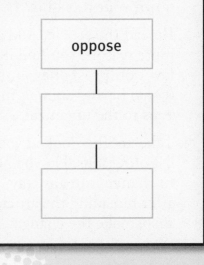

Add suffixes to the word *oppose* to create two other words in the same word family.

oppose

Prefix		Root		New Word	Word Meaning
op (means "against")	+	pos	=	oppose	to put against
ex (means "out")	+	pos	=	expose	
inter (means "between")	+	pos	=	interpose	

Write About It!

You have read an article about whether or not animals should be put in zoos. Now you will write about the topic. Read the writing prompt. It gives your writing assignment.

WRITING RUBRIC

In your response, you should:

- Write a blog expressing your opinion about zoos.

- Give reasons for your opinion based on the article.

- Use at least one word from the Word Bank.

- Use correct grammar, usage, and mechanics.

Writing Prompt

Imagine that you are going to write a blog posting on a Web site that is either for or against zoos. Write an e-mail paragraph giving your opinion on whether animals should be put in zoos. Use ideas from the article and at least one word from the Word Bank.
challenge • compromise • danger • disagreement • outcome

Prewrite It

Once you are sure you understand the prompt, plan what you want to say.

1. Review your notes from the class discussion. Use the organizer on the right to jot down your thoughts.

2. Reread the article. Add any more reasons you find in favor of (pros) or against (cons) having animals in zoos to the organizer.

3. Take another look at your list of reasons. Do you need to change it in any way after rereading the article? If so, make the changes.

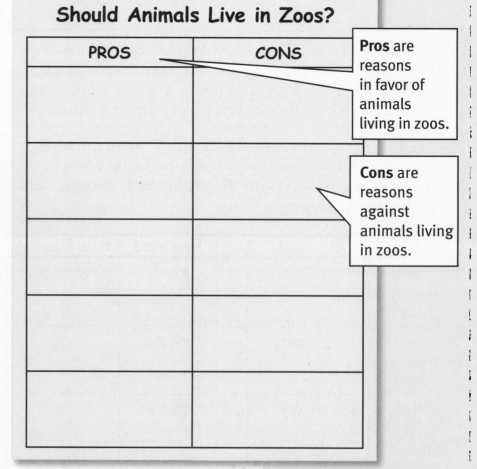

Should Animals Live in Zoos?

PROS	CONS

Pros are reasons in favor of animals living in zoos.

Cons are reasons against animals living in zoos.

Draft It

Now use your plan to draft, or write, your blog posting. The writing frame below will help you.

1. Start by giving your opinion. You have two choices of opinion. Underline your opinion.

2. Then give your reasons. Read the second sentence below. Finish the thought by giving a strong reason for your opinion. Explain your reason with ideas from the article.

Writing COACH

When writing a blog posting, try to stay focused. Many people do not read every sentence on a blog. You should only write about the most important points you want to make.

○ ○ ○

Animals in Zoos

I think that animals (do, do not) belong in zoos.

I think this because _____

_____

_____

_____

_____

_____

_____

_____

✔ **CHECKLIST**

Evaluate your writing. A score of "5" is excellent. A score of "1" means you need to do more work. Then ask a partner to rate your work.

1. **Does the blog e-mail clearly state an opinion about animals in zoos?**

   Me: 1 2 3 4 5
   Partner: 1 2 3 4 5

2. **Are there ideas from the article that explain the opinion?**

   Me: 1 2 3 4 5
   Partner: 1 2 3 4 5

3. **Is there at least one Word Bank word used?**

   Me: 1 2 3 4 5
   Partner: 1 2 3 4 5

4. **Are grammar, usage, and mechanics correct?**

   Me: 1 2 3 4 5
   Partner: 1 2 3 4 5

Check It and Fix It

After you have written your blog posting, check your work.

1. Is everything written clearly and correctly? Use the checklist on the right to see.

2. Read your speech out loud to a classmate. Talk over the reasons for your opinions. Use the ideas to revise your work.

3. For help with grammar, usage, and mechanics, go to the Handbook on pages 189–226.

Vocabulary Workshop

Add these words to your personal word bank by practicing them.

WORD BANK challenge • compromise • danger • disagreement • outcome

Define It

Fill in the chart with the Word Bank words. Tell what each word means. Then circle the number that tells how well you understand each word. Circle "4" if you understand it completely. Circle "1" if you are not sure you understand the word at all.

What It Means	challenge
	How Well I Understand It 1 2 3 4
What It Means	
	How Well I Understand It 1 2 3 4
What It Means	
	How Well I Understand It 1 2 3 4
What It Means	
	How Well I Understand It 1 2 3 4
What It Means	
	How Well I Understand It 1 2 3 4

A good way to remember new words is to use them to describe things from everyday life. Associating new words with real-life activities helps you picture what the words mean.

Show You Know

Answer the questions below to show you know how each boldface Word Bank word is used.

1. What is something you could do that would be a **challenge?** Why?

   _____

   _____

2. Teenagers and their parents often find themselves in **disagreement** about how to spend free time. Why?

   _____

   _____

3. If you do not study for a test, you might not be very happy with the **outcome**. Why?

   _____

   _____

Word Beginnings: *co-, com-*

- Prefixes tell something about the words that follow. The prefixes *co-* and *com-* mean "together." Using one of these prefixes means that the word that follows the prefix is or is done together.

- Add *co-* or *com-* to each word to make a new word. Then write the new word's meaning. Use the example below as a guide.

Original Word	New Word	Meaning
worker	co-worker	someone you work with
promised		
host		
operation		

Look through the article to find two other words in the same word family as *promise.*

promise

Write About It!

You have read an article about age limits. Now you will write about the topic. Read the writing prompt. It gives your writing assignment.

Writing Prompt

Imagine that you are going to write a letter to your state representative. Your letter should tell your opinion about whether the voting age should be lowered. Use ideas from the article and at least one word from the Word Bank.

communication • misunderstanding • resolution • struggle • subject

WRITING RUBRIC

In your response, you should:

- Write a letter about lowering the voting age.
- Give reasons for your opinion based on the article you read.
- Use at least one word from the Word Bank.
- Use correct grammar, usage, and mechanics.

Prewrite It

Once you are sure you understand the prompt, plan what you want to say.

1. Take a look at your notes from the class discussion. Use the organizer on the right to jot down your thoughts.

2. Reread the article. Look for additional reasons to support your opinion. Add these to your organizer.

3. Read your opinion again. Do you need to change it in any way after rereading the article? If so, make the changes. Read through the reasons you have listed. Which are the strongest? Cross out the reasons that are not as strong.

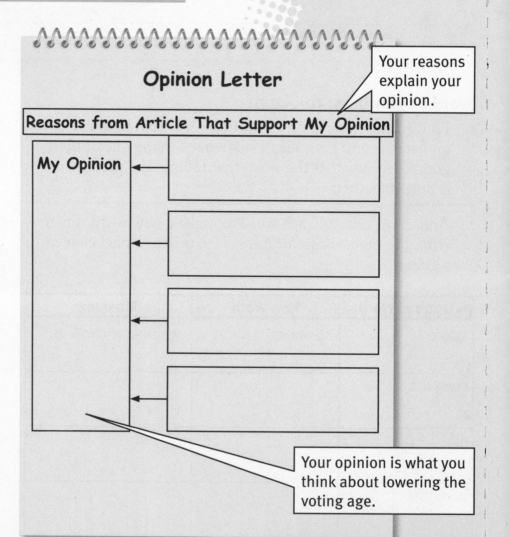

Opinion Letter

Your reasons explain your opinion.

Reasons from Article That Support My Opinion

My Opinion

Your opinion is what you think about lowering the voting age.

Draft It

Now use your plan to draft, or write, your letter. The writing frame below will help you.

1. Start by giving your opinion. You have two choices of opinion. Underline your opinion.

2. Then give your reasons. Read the second sentence below. Finish the thought by giving a strong reason for your opinion. Explain your reason with ideas from the article.

The strength of the reasons for your opinion has a lot to do with getting your reader to agree with you. Make sure to write the most important reason first.

Dear State Representative:

I think that the voting age (should, should not) be lowered to

16. I think this because _____

_____

_____

_____

_____

_____

_____

_____

_____

_____

_____

✔ CHECKLIST

Evaluate your writing.
A score of "5" is excellent.
A score of "1" means you need to do more work.
Then ask a partner to rate your work.

1. **Does the letter clearly state an opinion about lowering the voting age?**

   Me: 1 2 3 4 5
   Partner: 1 2 3 4 5

2. **Are there ideas from the article that explain the opinion?**

   Me: 1 2 3 4 5
   Partner: 1 2 3 4 5

3. **Is there at least one Word Bank word used?**

   Me: 1 2 3 4 5
   Partner: 1 2 3 4 5

4. **Are grammar, usage, and mechanics correct?**

   Me: 1 2 3 4 5
   Partner: 1 2 3 4 5

Check It and Fix It

After you have written your letter, check your work.

1. Is everything written clearly and correctly? Use the checklist on the right to see.

2. Then trade work with a classmate. Talk over ways you might improve your letters. Use the ideas to make changes to your work.

3. For help with grammar, usage, and mechanics, go to the Handbook on pages 189–226.

Vocabulary Workshop

Add these words to your personal word bank by practicing them.

WORD BANK communication • misunderstanding • resolution • struggle • subject

What other new words in the article would you like to remember? List them.

_____

_____

_____

Define It

Write what each word in the Word Bank means. Then think of a word that has the same or a very similar meaning.

What It Means	resolution
	A Word It Reminds Me Of _____
What It Means	
	A Word It Reminds Me Of _____
What It Means	
	A Word It Reminds Me Of _____
What It Means	
	A Word It Reminds Me Of _____
What It Means	
	A Word It Reminds Me Of _____

Show You Know

To show that you understand the Word Bank words, write a clue for each word. Exchange clues with a partner. See whether your partner can identify the correct word for each clue. Use the clue for the word *struggle* as a model.

- If you are having a hard time doing something but you keep on trying, you may be doing this.

1. _____

2. _____

3. _____

4. _____

5. _____

Word Sort

Sort the Word Bank words into the correct columns below. Read through the article and add your own words to each category. Use the examples as a guide.

Nouns	Verbs	Adjectives
communication struggle	struggle	

Now that you have sorted your words, pick two from different categories and combine them into a sentence. For a challenge, pick more than two and use them in a sentence.

1. _____

_____

2. _____

_____

UNIT 2 WRAP UP

Writing Reflection

Does every conflict have a winner?

Look through your writing from this unit and choose the best piece.
Reflect on this piece of writing by completing each sentence below.

My best piece of writing from this unit is _____

_____

I chose this piece because _____

_____

_____

While I was writing, one goal I had was _____

_____

I accomplished this goal by _____

_____

_____

This writing helped me think more about the Big Question because

_____

_____

One thing I learned while writing that can help me in the future is

_____

_____

Write About It!

You have read an article about Mars. Now you will write about the topic. Read the writing prompt. It gives your writing assignment.

Writing Prompt

After reading "Travel to Mars," you have some ideas about what life on Mars might be like. Imagine you are a pioneer in a colony on Mars. Write a postcard to a friend describing daily life on the planet. Use ideas from the article and at least one word from the Word Bank.

discover • explore • facts • organize • possible

WRITING RUBRIC

In your response, you should:

- Write a postcard to a friend describing your life on Mars.

- Give details about Mars based on the article.

- Use at least one word from the Word Bank.

- Use correct grammar, usage, and mechanics.

Prewrite It

Once you are sure you understand the prompt, plan what you want to say.

1. Review your notes from the class discussion. Use the web on the right to jot down your thoughts.

2. Reread the article. Look for more details about life on Mars. Add those to your web.

3. Take another look at your ideas. Do you need to add any after rereading the article? If so, make the changes. Then decide what details to include in your postcard to a friend.

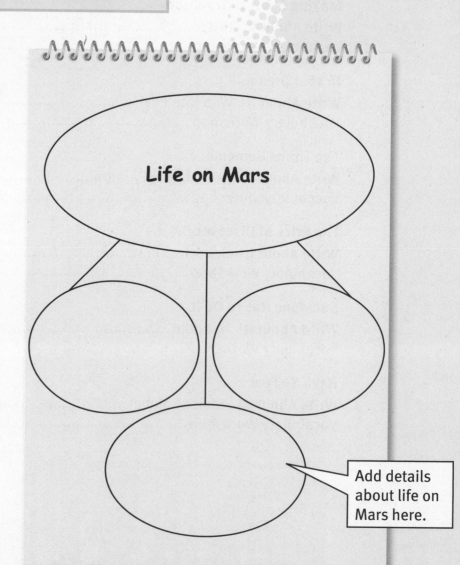

Life on Mars

Add details about life on Mars here.

Draft It

Now use your plan to draft, or write, a postcard to a friend. The writing frame below will help you.

1. Start by filling in the name of the person you are writing to. Then introduce the topic. You have three choices. Underline your choice.

2. Then give your description of life on Mars. Read the second sentence below. Finish the thought by giving details about your daily life. Make sure you include ideas from the article.

There is not much space to write on postcards. Make sure to include only the most important or interesting information.

Dear _____,

Life on Mars is (great, easy, hard). Daily life includes

_____

_____

_____

_____

_____

_____

_____

_____

Check It and Fix It

After you have written your postcard, check your work. Try to read it with a "fresh eye." Imagine that you have never read the postcard before.

1. Is everything written clearly and correctly? Use the checklist on the right to see.

2. Trade your work with a classmate. Talk over ways you both might improve your postcards. Use the ideas to revise your work.

3. For help with grammar, usage, and mechanics, go to the Handbook on pages 189–226.

✔ **CHECKLIST**

Evaluate your writing. A score of "5" is excellent. A score of "1" means you need to do more work. Then ask a partner to rate your work.

1. **Does the postcard describe daily life clearly?**

   Me: 1 2 3 4 5
   Partner: 1 2 3 4 5

2. **Are there ideas from the article that explain life on Mars?**

   Me: 1 2 3 4 5
   Partner: 1 2 3 4 5

3. **Is there at least one Word Bank word used?**

   Me: 1 2 3 4 5
   Partner: 1 2 3 4 5

4. **Are grammar, usage, and mechanics correct?**

   Me: 1 2 3 4 5
   Partner: 1 2 3 4 5

Vocabulary Workshop

Add these words to your personal word bank by practicing them.

WORD BANK discover • explore • facts • organize • possible

Define It

Fill in the chart with the Word Bank words. Tell what each word means. Then circle the number that tells how well you understand each word. Circle "4" if you understand it completely. Circle "1" if you are not sure you understand the word at all. Use the example as a model.

What It Means	discover	
To discover something is to find it for the first time.		**How Well I Understand It** 1 2 3 ④
What It Means		
		How Well I Understand It 1 2 3 4
What It Means		
		How Well I Understand It 1 2 3 4
What It Means		
		How Well I Understand It 1 2 3 4

Word COACH

One way to remember new words is to use them. Use new words in and out of class when you speak and write.

Show You Know

Answer the questions to show you know the meaning of each boldface Word Bank word.

1. Would you like to **discover** something or **explore** nature? Explain. _____

   _____

2. How can you **organize facts** when you write a report? _____

   _____

3. Name a goal that is **possible** for you to achieve on your own. _____

   _____

Word Beginnings: *im-*

- Adding a prefix to the beginning of a word changes the word's meaning. Adding *im-* to a word is like adding the word *not*.

  Positive Meaning: It is **possible** for me to make a basket.
  Negative Meaning: It is **impossible** for me to slam-dunk.

- Add *im-* to each boldface word and complete each sentence.

1. perfect

The tag said the shirt was _____, so we got 20 percent off.

2. personal

The invitation arrived via e-mail, which seemed _____ to me.

3. practical

Wearing shorts in the winter is an _____ choice.

4. mature

If you do not act your age, you may be called _____.

ALL IN THE FAMILY

The following words are in the same word family. What are some other words that have *possible* in them? Add two to the list.

possible
impossible

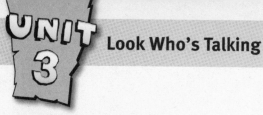

UNIT 3 — Look Who's Talking

Write About It!

You have read an article about communication. Now you will write about the topic. Read the writing prompt. It gives your writing assignment.

Writing Prompt

After reading "Look Who's Talking," do you think boys and girls speak differently? Imagine that you are a language expert. Design a checklist that you could use to listen for differences between boys and girls in conversation. Use ideas from the article and at least one word from the Word Bank.

analyze • investigate • question • topic • understand

Prewrite It

Once you are sure you understand the prompt, plan what you want to say.

1. Review your notes from the class discussion. Use the organizer on the right to jot down your thoughts.

2. Reread the article. Look for more similarities or differences between the speech of boys and girls. Add those to your organizer.

3. Take another look at your notes. Read through all the ideas you have listed. Which are the strongest? Cross out the ideas that are not as strong.

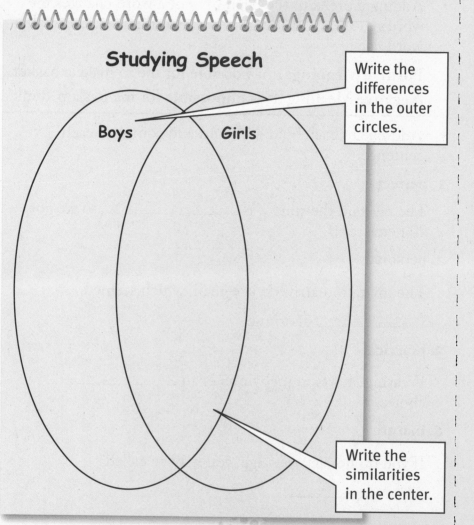

Studying Speech

Boys   Girls

Write the differences in the outer circles.

Write the similarities in the center.

Draft It

Now use your plan to draft, or write, a checklist. The writing frame below will help you.

1. Start by giving your opinion. You have three choices of opinion. Underline your choice.

2. Then give the differences you could listen for. Read the second sentence below. Finish the thought by creating a checklist. Make sure you base your ideas on facts from the article.

Most checklists are simple so that they are easy to use. The sentences in your checklist should be basic and to the point.

I think there are (many, a few, no) differences in the way boys and girls speak. I could use the following checklist to check my theory: _____

✓ _____

✓ _____

✓ _____

✓ _____

✓ _____

✓ _____

✓ _____

✓ _____

✓ _____

Check It and Fix It

After you have written your checklist, check your work. Imagine that you have never read the checklist before.

1. Is everything written clearly and correctly? Use the checklist on the right to see.

2. Trade your work with a classmate. Talk over ways to improve your checklists. Use the ideas to revise your work.

3. For help with grammar, usage, and mechanics, go to the Handbook on pages 189–226.

✔ **CHECKLIST**

Evaluate your writing. A score of "5" is excellent. A score of "1" means you need to do more work. Then ask a partner to rate your work.

1. **Does the checklist state differences I can see?**

   Me: 1 2 3 4 5
   Partner: 1 2 3 4 5

2. **Are there ideas from the article in the checklist?**

   Me: 1 2 3 4 5
   Partner: 1 2 3 4 5

3. **Is there at least one Word Bank word used?**

   Me: 1 2 3 4 5
   Partner: 1 2 3 4 5

4. **Are grammar, usage, and mechanics correct?**

   Me: 1 2 3 4 5
   Partner: 1 2 3 4 5

Vocabulary Workshop

Add these words to your personal word bank by practicing them.

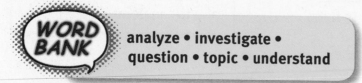

WORD BANK analyze • investigate • question • topic • understand

Your Choice

What other new words in the article would you like to remember? List them.

_____

_____

_____

Define It

Complete the graphic organizers below. Choose two Word Bank words that you could connect, and tell how the words are connected. You will use one word twice. Use the example as a model.

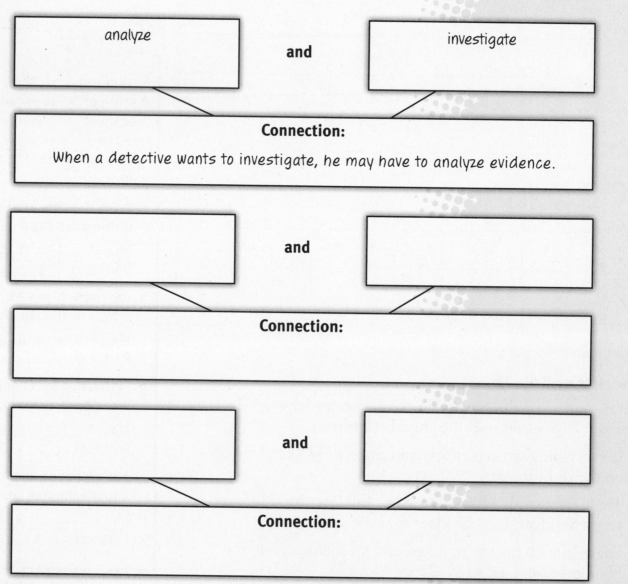

analyze	**and**	investigate

Connection:
When a detective wants to investigate, he may have to analyze evidence.

	and	

Connection:

	and	

Connection:

Show You Know

In the space below, write a short, short story (just a paragraph!) using the Word Bank words. Be sure your sentences show that you understand the meanings of the words.

Once upon a time _____

_____

_____

_____

_____

Partner Up

Read your story aloud to a partner. Have your partner suggest ways to make your story clearer.

Multiple-Meaning Words

- When you use a dictionary to find the meaning of a word, you often find more than one definition for the word. Which is the right one? Look at how the word is used in the context of a sentence. For example, which definition for *question* makes sense below?

  The coach seemed to **question** every call the referee made.

  question: (a) doubt the correctness of; (b) something asked

  If you chose definition (a), you are right. That definition makes sense in the sentence.

- Circle the correct meaning for each boldface word in the chart below.

Word in Sentence	Meaning 1	Meaning 2
Scientists **test** a theory by observing the weather.	to try out an idea	an exam
The **top** students will be invited to the awards ceremony.	a spinning toy	highest achievers
"Please read your **sentence** to the class," said the teacher.	a penalty	a string of words

Write About It!

You have read an article about Native Americans. Now you will write about the topic. Read the writing prompt. It gives your writing assignment.

Writing Prompt

A school in your community is considering naming a team after a Native American tribe. Write a letter to the school principal expressing whether or not you think this is a good idea. Use ideas from the article and at least one word from the Word Bank.

evaluate • inquire • interview • knowledge

WRITING RUBRIC

In your response, you should:

• Write a letter to the principal giving your opinion about the team name.

• Give reasons for your opinion based on the article you read.

• Use at least one word from the Word Bank.

• Use correct grammar, usage, and mechanics.

Prewrite It

Once you are sure you understand the prompt, plan what you want to say.

1. Review your notes from the class discussion. Use the organizer on the right to jot down your thoughts.

2. Reread the article. Look for additional reasons that support or explain your opinion. Add those to your organizer.

3. Take another look at your opinion. Do you need to change it in any way after rereading the article? If so, make the changes. Read through all the reasons you have listed. Which are the strongest? Cross out the reasons that are not as strong.

Letter to the Principal

My Opinion

> Your opinion is what you think about the issue.

My Reasons

> Your reasons explain your opinion.

Draft It

Now use your plan to draft, or write, a letter of opinion.
The writing frame below will help you.

1. Start by giving your opinion. You have three choices of opinion. Underline your opinion.

2. Then give your reasons. Read the second sentence below. Finish the thought by giving a strong reason for your opinion. Make sure you explain your reason with ideas from the article.

Read your letter to a partner. Are there parts of the letter that your partner does not understand? If so, you may need to revise your text to make it clearer.

Dear Principal:

I think naming your team after Native Americans is a(n)

(good, OK, bad) idea for your school. I think this because

_____

_____

_____

_____

_____

_____

_____

_____

_____

Check It and Fix It

After you have written your letter, check your work. Look at it with a "fresh eye," as if you have never read it before.

1. Is everything written clearly and correctly? Use the checklist on the right to see.

2. Trade your work with a classmate. Talk over ways you both might improve your letters. Use the ideas to revise your work.

3. For help with grammar, usage, and mechanics, go to the Handbook on pages 189–226.

✔ CHECKLIST

Evaluate your writing. A score of "5" is excellent. A score of "1" means you need to do more work. Then ask a partner to rate your work.

1. **Does the letter state the opinion clearly?**

   Me: 1 2 3 4 5
   Partner: 1 2 3 4 5

2. **Are there ideas from the article that explain the opinion?**

   Me: 1 2 3 4 5
   Partner: 1 2 3 4 5

3. **Is there at least one Word Bank word used?**

   Me: 1 2 3 4 5
   Partner: 1 2 3 4 5

4. **Are grammar, usage, and mechanics correct?**

   Me: 1 2 3 4 5
   Partner: 1 2 3 4 5

Vocabulary Workshop

Add these words to your personal word bank by practicing them.

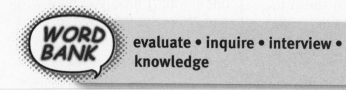 evaluate • inquire • interview • knowledge

Your Choice

What other new words in the article would you like to remember? List them.

_____

_____

_____

Define It

Complete the chart below. First, tell what the Word Bank word means. Then tell what the word does not mean. Use the example as a guide.

Word	What It Is	What It Is Not
evaluate	deciding whether something has value	adding or subtracting numbers
inquire		
interview		
knowledge		

Show You Know

Using all of the Word Bank words, write a dialogue between two characters. Make sure the dialogue shows that you understand the words' meanings.

_____ : _____

_____

_____ : _____

_____

_____ : _____

_____

_____ : _____

_____

Root *val*

- Learning the meanings of word roots can help you learn the meanings of new words. *Evaluate* is a Word Bank word that has the word root *val*, which means "to be worth."

- The following words are based on *val: value, valuable, evaluation,* and *invaluable.* Write the word that makes sense in each blank below.

1. This painting is rare and _____ and worth a lot of money.

2. Workers receive an _____ every year about their job skills.

3. The _____ of something tells what it is worth.

4. The study guide was _____ because it helped me learn.

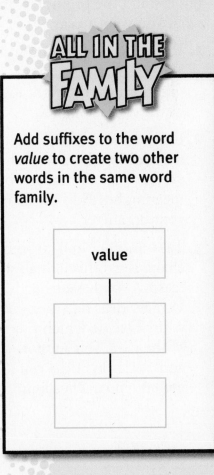

ALL IN THE FAMILY

Add suffixes to the word *value* to create two other words in the same word family.

value

UNIT **3** In Your Dreams

Write About It!

You have read an article about dreams. Now you will write about the topic. Read the writing prompt. It gives your writing assignment.

Writing Prompt

After reading "In Your Dreams," do you think dreams reveal hidden meanings? Imagine that you host a Web site about dreams. Respond to a post that asks whether or not dreams are meaningful. Use ideas from the article and at least one word from the Word Bank.
curiosity • examine • information • recall

Prewrite It

Once you are sure you understand the prompt, plan what you want to say.

1. Review your notes from the class discussion. Use the organizer on the right to jot down your thoughts.

2. Reread the article. Look for additional reasons why dreams may or may not be meaningful. Add those to your organizer.

3. Take another look at your chart. Read through all the reasons you have listed. Which ideas do you agree with? Decide which side of the issue you support and circle the ideas you'll include in your response.

RUBRIC

In your response, you should:

• Tell whether or not you think dreams are meaningful.

• Give reasons for your opinion based on the article you read.

• Use at least one word from the Word Bank.

• Use correct grammar, usage, and mechanics.

Dreams

Dreams are meaningful because…	Dreams are not meaningful because…

Writing Journal

© Pearson Education, Inc. All rights reserved.

Draft It

Now use your plan to draft, or write, a post for your Web site. The writing frame below will help you.

1. Start by giving your opinion. You have two choices of opinion. Underline your opinion.

2. Then give your reasons. Read the second sentence below. Finish the thought by giving a strong reason for your opinion. Then list more reasons. Make sure you explain your reasons with ideas from the article.

Mention the strongest reason that supports your opinion near the top of the post. Then continue with the second strongest, the third strongest, and so on. Do not include any weak reason in the post.

Dear Dreamer,

I think dreams (are, are not) meaningful. I think

this because _____

_____

_____

_____

_____

_____

_____

_____

Check It and Fix It

After you have written your post, check your work. Read it using a fresh way of looking at it. Imagine that you have never read the post before.

1. Is everything written clearly and correctly? Use the checklist on the right to see.

2. Trade your work with a classmate. Talk over ways you might improve your responses. Use the ideas to revise your work.

3. For help with grammar, usage, and mechanics, go to the Handbook on pages 189–226.

 CHECKLIST

Evaluate your writing.
A score of "5" is excellent.
A score of "1" means you need to do more work.
Then ask a partner to rate your work.

1. **Does the post state the opinion clearly?**

   Me: 1 2 3 4 5
   Partner: 1 2 3 4 5

2. **Are there ideas from the article that support the post?**

   Me: 1 2 3 4 5
   Partner: 1 2 3 4 5

3. **Is there at least one Word Bank word used?**

   Me: 1 2 3 4 5
   Partner: 1 2 3 4 5

4. **Are grammar, usage, and mechanics correct?**

   Me: 1 2 3 4 5
   Partner: 1 2 3 4 5

Vocabulary Workshop

Add these words to your personal word bank by practicing them.

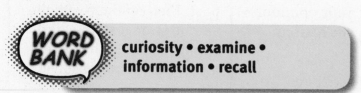

WORD BANK · curiosity • examine • information • recall

Define It

Choose two words from the Word Bank and explain how they are connected. Write the first word on the left side. Write the second word on the right side. Write your explanation under the words. Repeat the process with the remaining Word Bank words. Use the example as a guide.

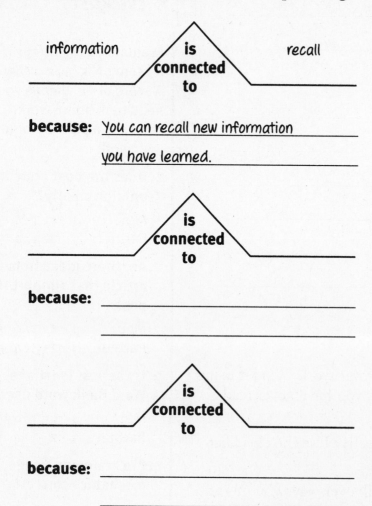

information   **is connected to**   recall

because: You can recall new information you have learned.

is connected to

because: _____

_____

is connected to

because: _____

_____

Word COACH

A good way to remember new words is to make connections. Think of an experience you have had that you could connect with a new word. A new word could also remind you of a word you already know.

Show You Know

To show that you understand the words, write one clue for each word in the Word Bank. Exchange clues with a partner and see if your partner can identify the correct word for each clue. See the example for the word *examine*.

• You might do this with a microscope.

1. _____

2. _____

3. _____

4. _____

Word Endings: *-ity, -ty*

• When you add the word ending *-ity* or *-ty* to a word, you change the word from an adjective to a noun.

Adjective: The **curious** kitten tumbled into the bag of yarn.

Noun: The **curiosity** of animals leads them to new places.

• Add *-ity* or *-ty* to the boldface words below to fill in the blanks.

1. similar

Due to our _____, people often call me by my sister's name.

2. royal

I wonder what it would be like to be treated like

_____.

3. cruel

The actor played the part with a _____ that seemed real.

4. loyal

_____ is a quality I value in others.

These words belong to the same word family. Highlight the suffix on each word. For an extra challenge, tell each word's part of speech.

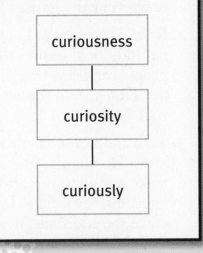

curiousness

curiosity

curiously

Write About It!

You have read an article about the Titans football team. Now you will write about the topic. Read the writing prompt. It gives your writing assignment.

Writing Prompt

After reading "The Titans Remember," you know more about the lessons people can learn from those who are different. Think about the lessons of the Titans. Write a paragraph explaining one lesson people can learn from the Titans. Use ideas from the article and at least one word from the Word Bank.

analyze • background • facts • interview • understand

WRITING RUBRIC

In your response, you should:

• Write a paragraph that explains a lesson people can learn from the Titans.

• Include supporting ideas from the article you read.

• Use at least one word from the Word Bank.

• Use correct grammar, usage, and mechanics.

Prewrite It

Once you are sure you understand the prompt, plan what you want to say.

1. Review your notes from the class discussion. Use the organizer on the right to jot down your thoughts.

2. Reread the article. Look for additional lessons that people can learn from the Titans. Add those to your organizer.

3. Take another look at your ideas. Do you need to make any additions after rereading the article? If so, make the additions. Read through all the lessons and circle the one you will write about in your paragraph.

Learning from the Titans

Lessons

Make a list of lessons to learn from the Titans.

Draft It

Now use your plan to draft, or write, a paragraph. The writing frame below will help you.

1. Start by stating the lesson you will explain. Write the lesson by completing the first sentence.

2. Then give your explanation. Read the second sentence below. Finish the thought by giving your explanation of the lesson. Make sure you include supporting ideas from the article.

The most important lesson to learn from the Titans is

_____

_____ .

This lesson is important because _____

_____

_____

_____

_____

_____

_____

_____

Work with a partner to finish your paragraph. After deciding which lesson is most important, make a list of the reasons you think support your opinion. Your partner might come up with reasons you had not thought of yourself.

Check It and Fix It

After you have written your paragraph, check your work with a "fresh eye." Imagine that you have never read the paragraph before.

1. Is everything written clearly and correctly? Use the checklist on the right to see.

2. Trade your work with a classmate. Talk over ways you both might improve your paragraphs. Use the ideas to revise your work.

3. For help with grammar, usage, and mechanics, go to the Handbook on pages 189–226.

✔ **CHECKLIST**

Evaluate your writing. A score of "5" is excellent. A score of "1" means you need to do more work. Then ask a partner to rate your work.

1. **Does the paragraph state the lesson clearly?**

   Me: 1 2 3 4 5
   Partner: 1 2 3 4 5

2. **Are there ideas from the article that explain the lesson?**

   Me: 1 2 3 4 5
   Partner: 1 2 3 4 5

3. **Is there at least one Word Bank word used?**

   Me: 1 2 3 4 5
   Partner: 1 2 3 4 5

4. **Are grammar, usage, and mechanics correct?**

   Me: 1 2 3 4 5
   Partner: 1 2 3 4 5

Vocabulary Workshop

Add these words to your personal word bank by practicing them.

WORD BANK

analyze • background • facts • interview • understand

Your Choice

What other new words in the article would you like to remember? List them.

_____

_____

_____

Define It

Complete the chart below. Write each Word Bank word and tell what it means. Then write a word you know that reminds you of the new word.

What It Means	analyze
to examine carefully	**A Word It Reminds Me Of** study
What It Means	
	A Word It Reminds Me Of _____
What It Means	
	A Word It Reminds Me Of _____
What It Means	
	A Word It Reminds Me Of _____
What It Means	
	A Word It Reminds Me Of _____

Show You Know

In the space below, write a short, short story (just a paragraph!) using the Word Bank words. Be sure your sentences show that you understand the meanings of the words.

Once upon a time _____

_____

_____

_____

_____

_____

_____

Partner Up

Trade the short, short story you wrote with a partner. Go over any part of the story that is unclear to your partner and revise it to make it clearer. Then make any other necessary corrections.

Compound Words

- When you put two words together to make a new word, you create a compound word. You can divide a compound word into the parts that make it up to help you understand it. For example, *background* is a Word Bank word made up of the words *back* and *ground*.

- Use the words below to make compound words. Then use the new compound words to complete the sentences.

   maker • school • foot • back • mate • film • ball • team • quarter • house

1. I want to play the position of _____ on the _____ team.

2. You must work together with every _____ to win games!

3. Who was the _____ who directed the *Star Wars* movies?

4. Students of all grades attended class in a one-room _____.

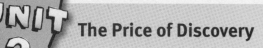

Write About It!

You have read an article about the U.S. space program. Now you will write about the topic. Read the writing prompt. It gives your writing assignment.

Writing Prompt

You have been asked to take part in a student debate. Do you think the high cost of space exploration is worth it? Write a speech explaining whether or not you think the space program is worth the cost. Use ideas from the article and at least one word from the Word Bank.

examine • experiment • explore • investigate

WRITING RUBRIC

In your response, you should:

- Write a speech expressing your opinion about the space program.

- Give reasons for your opinion based on the article you read.

- Use at least one word from the Word Bank.

- Use correct grammar, usage, and mechanics.

Prewrite It

Once you are sure you understand the prompt, plan what you want to say.

1. Review your notes from the class discussion. Use the organizer on the right to jot down your thoughts.

2. Reread the article. Look for additional reasons for and against the cost of the space program. Add those to your organizer.

3. Take another look at your opinion. Read through all the reasons you have listed. Which ideas do you agree with? Decide which side of the issue you support and circle the ideas you will include in your speech.

Space Exploration

The cost of the space program is worth it because...	The cost of the space program is not worth it because...

Draft It

Now use your plan to draft, or write, a speech. The writing frame below will help you.

1. Start by giving your opinion. You have two choices of opinion. Underline your opinion.

2. Then give your reasons. Read the second sentence below. Finish the thought by giving a strong reason for your opinion. Make sure you explain your reason with ideas from the article.

When writing a speech, try to include facts a speaker could show by using a visual aid. Visual aids, such as charts and graphs, make speeches more interesting to listeners.

I believe the space program (is, is not) worth the cost. I think

this because _____

_____

_____

_____

_____

_____

_____

_____

_____

_____

_____

_____

Check It and Fix It

After you have written your speech, check your work. Try to read the speech as if you have never read it before.

1. Is everything written clearly and correctly? Use the checklist on the right to see.

2. Trade your work with a classmate. Talk over ways you both might improve your speeches. Use the ideas to revise your work.

3. For help with grammar, usage, and mechanics, go to the Handbook on pages 189–226.

✔ CHECKLIST

Evaluate your writing.
A score of "5" is excellent.
A score of "1" means you need to do more work.
Then ask a partner to rate your work.

1. **Does the speech state the opinion clearly?**

   Me: 1 2 3 4 5
   Partner: 1 2 3 4 5

2. **Are there ideas from the article that explain the opinion?**

   Me: 1 2 3 4 5
   Partner: 1 2 3 4 5

3. **Is there at least one Word Bank word used?**

   Me: 1 2 3 4 5
   Partner: 1 2 3 4 5

4. **Are grammar, usage, and mechanics correct?**

   Me: 1 2 3 4 5
   Partner: 1 2 3 4 5

Vocabulary Workshop

Add these words to your personal word bank by practicing them.

 examine • experiment • explore • investigate

Your Choice

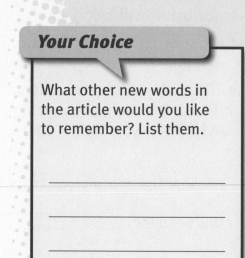

What other new words in the article would you like to remember? List them.

_____

_____

_____

Define It

Complete the chart below with words from the Word Bank. In the center oval, write two or three subjects you could write about using these four words.

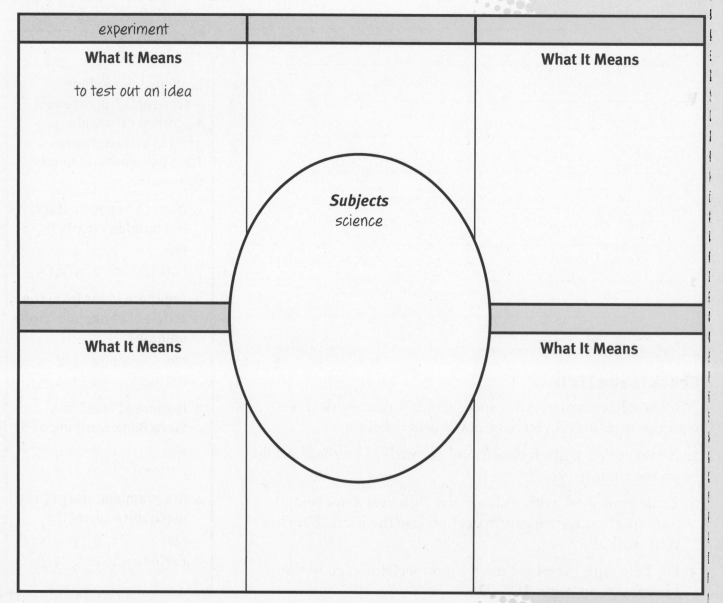

experiment

What It Means

to test out an idea

What It Means

Subjects
science

What It Means

What It Means

Show You Know

Complete the questions below to show you know how each boldface Word Bank word is used.

1. Whose job is it to **examine** a patient's arm to determine if it is broken?

   _____

2. Name three items you might use in a science **experiment**.

   _____

   _____

3. Name an area where you would like to **explore** the wilderness.

   _____

Word Endings: *-ation*

- When you add the word ending *-ation* to a word, you make a new word that is a noun.

   Verb: I want to **explore** the woods behind my house.
   Noun: I gave a report on our space **exploration** program.

- Add *-ation* to each boldface word to complete each sentence with a noun.

1. imagine

   Use your _____ to help you write a story.

2. organize

   _____ will help us keep our classroom tidy.

3. examine

   My brother took an _____ to get into college.

Partner Up

Trade questions and answers with a partner. Compare answers and discuss any other possible responses. If something needs to be corrected, make the changes.

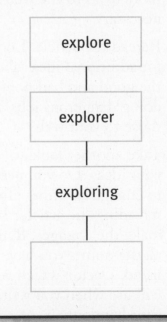

These words are part of the same word family. What are some other words that have the word *explore* in them? Add one to the list.

explore
explorer
exploring

UNIT 3

Someone Has to Do It

Write About It!

You have read an article about dangerous jobs. Now you will write about the topic. Read the writing prompt. It gives your writing assignment.

Writing Prompt

Imagine that your school is planning a career day. You have been asked to work at the "Dirty Jobs" table. Write a handout defining dirty jobs and giving an example of one. Include good points and bad points about the dirty job. Use ideas from the article and at least one word from the Word Bank.

curiosity • discipline • discover • inquire • question

Prewrite It

Once you are sure you understand the prompt, plan what you want to say.

1. Review your notes from the class discussion. Use the organizer on the right to jot down your thoughts. Add more ovals to the web if necessary.

2. Reread the article. Look for additional ideas about the good and bad points of doing dangerous jobs. Add those to your web.

3. Take another look at your ideas. Do you need to change anything after rereading the article? If so, make the changes. Reread all the points you have listed. Decide which you will use when you write your handout.

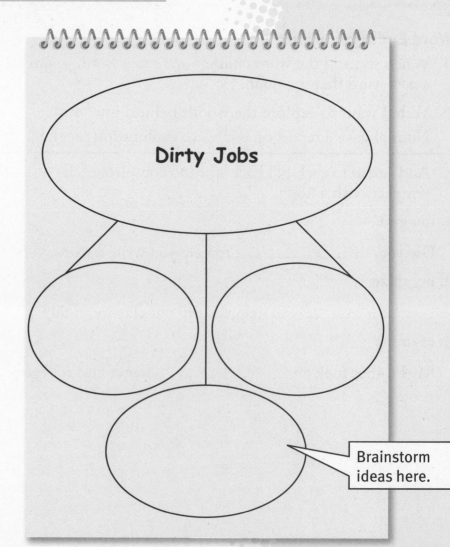

Dirty Jobs

Brainstorm ideas here.

Draft It

Now use your plan to draft, or write, a handout. The writing frame below will help you.

1. Start by defining *dirty job*.

2. Then give an example of a dirty job. Read the second sentence below. Finish the thought by giving an example. Then describe good points and bad points about the job. Base your points on ideas from the article.

Discuss jobs and responsibilities around the school with a partner. Decide which might be considered dirty jobs. This can help you figure out what to include in your handout.

What Is a Dirty Job?	
Dirty job may be defined as _____ _____ _____	
An example of a dirty job is _____	

Good Points of the Dirty Job	Bad Points of the Dirty Job
_____	_____
_____	_____
_____	_____
_____	_____
_____	_____
_____	_____

Check It and Fix It

After you have written your handout, check your work. Try to look at it with a "fresh eye."

1. Is everything written clearly and correctly? Use the checklist on the right to see.

2. Trade your work with a classmate. Talk over ways you both might improve your handouts. Use the ideas to revise your work.

3. For help with grammar, usage, and mechanics, go to the Handbook on pages 189–226.

✔ CHECKLIST

Evaluate your writing. A score of "5" is excellent. A score of "1" means you need to do more work. Then ask a partner to rate your work.

1. Does the handout define *dirty job* clearly?

Me: 1 2 3 4 5
Partner: 1 2 3 4 5

2. Are there ideas from the article represented in the good points and bad points?

Me: 1 2 3 4 5
Partner: 1 2 3 4 5

3. Is there at least one Word Bank word used?

Me: 1 2 3 4 5
Partner: 1 2 3 4 5

4. Are grammar, usage, and mechanics correct?

Me: 1 2 3 4 5
Partner: 1 2 3 4 5

Vocabulary Workshop

Add these words to your personal word bank by practicing them.

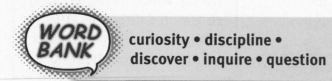

WORD BANK curiosity • discipline • discover • inquire • question

Define It

Complete the chart below. Write each Word Bank word and what it means. Then circle the number that shows how well you understand the word.

What It Means	curiosity
	How Well I Understand It 1 2 3 4
What It Means	
	How Well I Understand It 1 2 3 4
What It Means	
	How Well I Understand It 1 2 3 4
What It Means	
	How Well I Understand It 1 2 3 4
What It Means	
	How Well I Understand It 1 2 3 4

Your Choice

What other new words in the article would you like to remember? List them.

_____

_____

_____

Word COACH

How can you tell whether you understand a Word Bank word? See if you can explain what it means without looking back at the Word Bank definition.

Show You Know

To show that you understand the meaning of the words, write one clue for each word in the Word Bank. Exchange clues with a partner and see if your partner can identify the correct word for each clue. Use the sample clue for the word *curiosity* as a model.

• Nosy people are filled with this quality.

1. _____

2. _____

3. _____

4. _____

5. _____

Context Clues

• Nearby words and sentences may reveal clues to an unknown word's meaning. These are context clues. Notice how the underlined context clues below help define *discipline* as a field, or profession.

People may choose risky <u>jobs</u> to <u>avoid being in an office</u> all day. Some people want a **discipline** that lets them <u>be active or outdoors.</u>

_____

• Underline context clues in each sentence and define the boldface word.

1. The **loggers** spent their day cutting down trees and stacking logs.

_____

2. The drivers will **transport** the logs to different places, including distant countries.

_____

3. Because they work with power lines that carry electricity, electrical workers are at risk of being **electrocuted.**

_____

Write About It!

You have read an article about phobias. Now you will write about the topic. Read the writing prompt. It gives your writing assignment.

WRITING RUBRIC

In your response, you should:

- Write a letter giving your advice for overcoming fear.

- Use ideas from the article to give ways to overcome fears.

- Use at least one word from the Word Bank.

- Use correct grammar, usage, and mechanics.

Writing Prompt

After reading "Have No Fear," what advice would you give someone who was afraid of spiders? Imagine that you write an advice column. Write a letter responding to a student who has asked how to overcome the fear of spiders. Use ideas from the article and at least one word from the Word Bank.

approach • evaluate • experiment • information • knowledge

Prewrite It

Once you are sure you understand the prompt, plan what you want to say.

1. Review your notes from the class discussion. Use the organizer on the right to jot down your thoughts.

2. Reread the article. Look for more ways to overcome the fear of spiders. Add those to your organizer.

3. Take another look at your list. Do you need to change it in any way after rereading the article? If so, make the changes. Reread all the ideas you have listed. Which are the strongest? Cross out the ideas that are not as strong.

Asking for Advice

Ways to Overcome Fear

1. _____

_____

2. _____

_____

3. _____

_____

4. _____

_____

5. _____

_____

Draft It

Now use your plan to draft, or write, a letter giving advice. The writing frame below will help you.

1. Start by giving your advice. You have three choices your letter may support. Underline your choice.

2. Then give the ways you recommend to overcome fear. Read the second sentence below. Finish the thought by writing about what you think works best. Make sure you explain your advice with ideas from the article.

There are many tips in the article on ways to overcome fear. Which tip do you think would be the most effective? Base your letter around that tip.

Dear Reader,

There are (many, some, a few) ways to overcome your fear of

spiders. I recommend that you _____

_____

_____

_____

_____

_____

_____

_____

_____

✔ CHECKLIST

Evaluate your writing. A score of "5" is excellent. A score of "1" means you need to do more work. Then ask a partner to rate your work.

1. **Does the letter state the advice clearly?**

   Me: 1   2   3   4   5
   Partner: 1   2   3   4   5

2. **Are there ideas from the article that explain the advice?**

   Me: 1   2   3   4   5
   Partner: 1   2   3   4   5

3. **Is there at least one Word Bank word used?**

   Me: 1   2   3   4   5
   Partner: 1   2   3   4   5

4. **Are grammar, usage, and mechanics correct?**

   Me: 1   2   3   4   5
   Partner: 1   2   3   4   5

Check It and Fix It

After you have written your letter, check your work. Try to read it from a fresh perspective. Imagine that you have never read the letter before.

1. Is everything written clearly and correctly? Use the checklist on the right to see.

2. Trade your work with a classmate. Talk over ways you both might improve your letters. Use the ideas to revise your work.

3. For help with grammar, usage, and mechanics, go to the Handbook on pages 189–226.

Vocabulary Workshop

Add these words to your personal word bank by practicing them.

WORD BANK approach • evaluate • experiment • information • knowledge

Your Choice

What other new words in the article would you like to remember? List them.

_____

_____

_____

Define It

Complete the chart below using Word Bank words. Write the word in the first column. In the second column, give a real-life example of the word. In the third column, write your connection to the word. Use the example as a guide.

Word	Real-Life Example	My Connection
approach	I ask to pet a friend's dog before I approach the dog.	Walking in someone's direction is a way to approach a person.

Show You Know

Write a comic strip in the space below using all of the Word Bank words. Make sure the comic strip shows that you understand the words' meanings.

Partner Up

Trade comic strips with a partner. Read through each other's comic strips silently, and then read each aloud. Revise any language that is unclear.

Word Endings: -al

- When you add the word ending -al to a word, you create a new word that is an adjective.

   Noun: We are planning to finish the **experiment** today.
   Adjective: This is an **experimental** procedure that might not work.

- Add the ending -al to each boldface word below to create an adjective and complete the sentence. Write the new word in the blank.

1. There was a terrible car **accident** on the highway.

   The driver's mistake was _____.

2. Many people recycle in order to help the **environment.**

   My brother is interested in studying _____ science.

3. Be careful not to put too many plugs into that **electric** outlet.

   Overloading an outlet might cause an _____ problem.

4. The leaders of the **industry** got together for a meeting.

   There are many factories in the _____ part of town.

Writing Reflection

What should we learn?

Look through your writing from this unit and choose the best piece. Reflect on this piece of writing by completing each sentence below.

My best piece of writing from this unit is _____

_____

I chose this piece because _____

_____

_____

While I was writing, one goal I had was _____

_____

I accomplished this goal by _____

_____

_____

This writing helped me think more about the Big Question because

_____

_____

One thing I learned while writing that can help me in the future is

_____

_____

UNIT 4

❓ What is the best way to communicate?

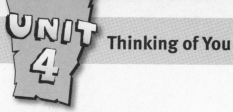

Write About It!

You have read an article about greeting cards. Now you will write about the topic. Read the writing prompt. It gives your writing assignment.

Writing Prompt

Imagine that you and a friend had a misunderstanding a few days ago. Would you send an apology in a greeting card, an e-card, or a different form of communication? In a paragraph or two, explain which form of communication you think would be best and why. Use ideas from the article and at least one word from the Word Bank.

enrich • entertain • express • produce • translate

WRITING RUBRIC

In your response, you should:

- Write one or two paragraphs.

- Use details from the article to explain why you would choose a particular form of communication.

- Use at least one word from the Word Bank.

- Use correct grammar, usage, and mechanics.

Prewrite It

Once you are sure you understand the prompt, plan what you want to say.

1. Review your notes from the class discussion. In the organizer, write notes about each type of communication.

2. Reread the article. Look for additional details about the types of communication. The details should include both pros and cons. Write those details in the organizer.

3. Look in your organizer for the column that has the most pros. Cross out the other two columns. In the column you chose, circle the ideas you want to include in your writing.

Forms of Communicating

Greeting Card	E-card	Other: _____

Draft It

Now use your plan to draft, or write, your paragraphs. The writing frame below will help you.

1. Start by underlining the form of communication you would choose for your apology.

2. The rest of your writing should give reasons for your choice. Begin with your strongest reason.

Try to show your audience why your choice makes sense. Be sure to support your opinion with facts from the article.

To apologize to a friend, I would choose (a greeting card, an

e-card, something else). One reason for this choice is

_____

_____

_____

_____

_____

_____

_____

_____

_____

_____

_____

✔ CHECKLIST

Evaluate your writing.
A score of "5" is excellent.
A score of "1" means you need to do more work.
Then ask a partner to rate your work.

1. Does the writing explain why a certain form of communication is best?

Me: 1 2 3 4 5
Partner: 1 2 3 4 5

2. Does the writing include details from the article?

Me: 1 2 3 4 5
Partner: 1 2 3 4 5

3. Is there at least one Word Bank word used?

Me: 1 2 3 4 5
Partner: 1 2 3 4 5

4. Are grammar, usage, and mechanics correct?

Me: 1 2 3 4 5
Partner: 1 2 3 4 5

Check It and Fix It

After you have finished writing, check your work. Read your writing aloud to a partner to see if it sounds convincing.

1. Is everything written clearly and correctly? Use the checklist on the right to see.

2. Trade paragraphs with a classmate. Talk over ways you might improve your paragraphs. Use the ideas to revise your work.

3. For help with grammar, usage, and mechanics, go to the Handbook on pages 189–226.

Vocabulary Workshop

Add these words to your personal word bank by practicing them.

 **WORD BANK** enrich • entertain • express • produce • translate

Define It

Complete the chart below. First, give a real-life example of the word. Then, tell your connection to the word. Use the example as a guide.

Word	Real-Life Example	My Connection to the Word
enrich	I tried to enrich my musical knowledge by taking a voice class.	I eat cereal enriched with vitamins.
entertain		
express		
produce		
translate		

Show You Know

To show that you understand the Word Bank words, write them in three sentences. In each sentence, use and highlight two of the words. You will use one word twice. Use the example as a model.

- Music can entertain people, but it can also express feelings.

1. _____

   _____

2. _____

   _____

3. _____

   _____

Partner Up

Trade sentences with a partner. Check the sentences to see if the words are used correctly. If a word is used incorrectly, discuss how to revise the sentence it is in. Then make the corrections.

Prefix: *trans-*

- Many words that begin with the prefix *trans-* relate to the meaning "across" or "so as to change." *Translate* means "to change from one language to another." *Transmit* means "to send across from one person or place to another."

- Complete each sentence by writing the correct word in the blank.

transatlantic • transfer • transform • translate • transmit

What do you think is the best way to _____ a message from one person to another? Even if a friend lives across the ocean in Europe, you can send _____ communication! A happy message can _____ your friend's mood. Using a computer is one way to _____ a greeting. If you can connect to a camera, that is even better. A smile is a greeting that no one needs to _____.

ALL IN THE FAMILY

Add suffixes to the word *translate* to create two other words in the same word family.

translate

UNIT 4

Word on the Wire

Write About It!

You have read an article about cell phones. Now you will write about the topic. Read the writing prompt. It gives your writing assignment.

Writing Prompt

What do you think about cell phones and their uses? Write a short student guide to responsible cell phone use. In your guide, include possible benefits and drawbacks of talking and texting on a cell phone. Use ideas from the article and at least one word from the Word Bank.

communicate • listen • prepare • technology • transmit

Prewrite It

Once you are sure you understand the prompt, plan what you want to say.

1. Review your notes from the class discussion. In the organizer, jot down both benefits and drawbacks of cell phones.

2. Reread the article. Look for more details about cell phone benefits and drawbacks and add them to the organizer.

3. Remember that your writing is aimed at students who use cell phones. Look at your organizer to decide which details will be most important for your readers. Circle those details to be sure you include them.

Cell Phones: Talking and Texting

Benefits	Drawbacks

Draft It

Now use your plan to write your guide. The writing frame below will help you.

1. Start with a statement about responsible cell phone use. You have three choices of opinion. Underline your choice.

2. To support your opinion, write about the benefits of using cell phones. Then include some of the drawbacks. Make sure to use ideas from the article in your guide.

Read your guide aloud to a partner. Does the guide tell how to use cell phones responsibly? If not, discuss ways to revise the guide to make it more useful. Then make the changes.

Students should use cell phones (whenever they want, only in certain situations, for emergencies only). Some of the benefits of using cell phones in this way are _____

_____

_____

_____

_____

_____

_____

_____

Check It and Fix It

After you have written your guide, check your work. Read with a "fresh eye" to make sure it makes sense. Look for any mistakes.

1. Is everything written clearly and correctly? Use the checklist on the right to see.

2. Trade your work with a classmate. Talk over ways to improve your guides. Use the ideas to revise your work.

3. For help with grammar, usage, and mechanics, go to the Handbook on pages 189–226.

✔ CHECKLIST

Evaluate your writing. A score of "5" is excellent. A score of "1" means you need to do more work. Then ask a partner to rate your work.

1. **Does the guide offer valuable information about responsible cell phone use?**

   Me: 1 2 3 4 5
   Partner: 1 2 3 4 5

2. **Does the writing include details from the article?**

   Me: 1 2 3 4 5
   Partner: 1 2 3 4 5

3. **Is there at least one Word Bank word used?**

   Me: 1 2 3 4 5
   Partner: 1 2 3 4 5

4. **Are grammar, usage, and mechanics correct?**

   Me: 1 2 3 4 5
   Partner: 1 2 3 4 5

Vocabulary Workshop

Add these words to your personal word bank by practicing them.

 **WORD BANK** communicate • listen • prepare • technology • transmit

Define It

Choose two words from the Word Bank and write them in the small boxes below. In the "Connection" box, describe how the two words are connected. Do this for three sets of words. One word will be used twice.

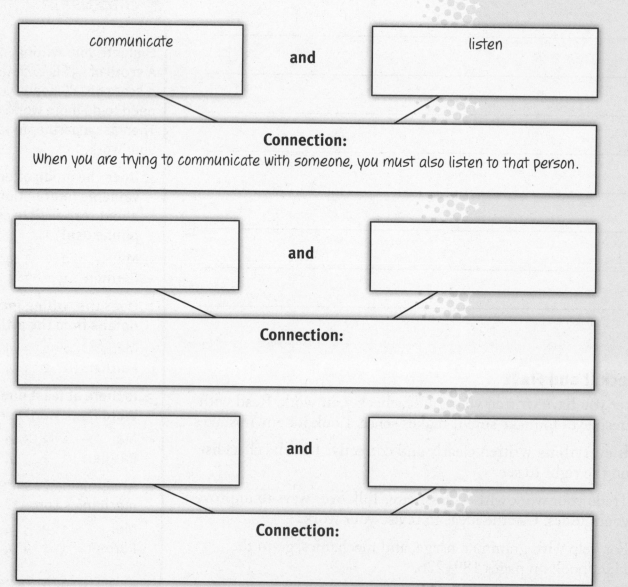

| communicate | and | listen |

Connection:
When you are trying to communicate with someone, you must also listen to that person.

| | and | |

Connection:

| | and | |

Connection:

Show You Know

For each word from the Word Bank, write a clue sentence for a partner to see if he or she can match it with the correct term. Use the clue for the word *communicate* as a model.

• This is something you can do to deliver a message.

1. _____

2. _____

3. _____

4. _____

5. _____

Prefix That Means "Before": *pre-*

• Many words that begin with *pre-* relate to the meaning "before." *Prepare* means "to make or do something in advance." *Predict* means "to tell what is going to happen, based on what has happened before."

• Adding *pre-* to words changes their meaning. *Preschool* is a school that children attend before going to kindergarten or elementary school.

• Write the correct words in the blanks to complete each sentence.

precaution • predict • prejudge • prepay • previews

Long ago, it would have been hard to _____ how cell phones would change people's lives. I try not to _____ people who speak loudly on the phone at the movie theater, but those people can ruin the _____! My parents _____ my bill so that I have a limited number of minutes. Having a cell phone is a great _____ in case of an emergency.

Change the ending of the word *prepare* to *-ed* and *-ation* to make a word family. How do these endings change the meaning of the word?

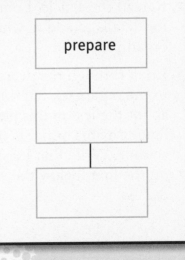

prepare

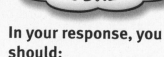

UNIT 4 A Show of Strength

Write About It!

You have read an article about people who became heroes. Now you will write about the topic. Read the writing prompt. It gives your writing assignment.

WRITING RUBRIC

In your response, you should:

- Write a short feature for a newspaper.
- Use details from the article in your writing.
- Use at least one word from the Word Bank.
- Use correct grammar, usage, and mechanics.

Writing Prompt

Write a short feature article for a school newspaper on one of the heroes described in "A Show of Strength." In your article, explain what lesson you think the hero communicated through his or her actions. Use ideas from the article and at least one word from the Word Bank.

contribute • inform • react • source • speak

Prewrite It

Once you are sure you understand the prompt, plan what you want to write.

1. Review your notes from the class discussion. Choose a hero from the article and start writing details in the organizer.

2. Reread the article. Look for details to add to your organizer.

3. Look through the details in the organizer and think about the lesson this person taught by his or her heroic actions. Write that lesson on the lines below the details.

Who is the hero?	
What did the hero do?	
When and where did these actions happen?	
Why did the hero do them?	

Through these actions, this hero showed that

_____

_____

_____

_____

_____

_____

_____

Draft It

Now use your plan to draft, or write, your article. The writing frame below will help you.

1. Start by writing who the hero is and what he or she did.

2. Then use details you listed in the chart to explain what happened. At the end of the article, write the lesson the hero communicated.

Hero Shows Great Courage

_____
(Name of hero)

became a hero when _____

_____

_____

_____

_____

_____

This hero showed that _____

_____

_____

_____ .

CHECKLIST

Evaluate your writing. A score of "5" is excellent. A score of "1" means you need to do more work. Then ask a partner to rate your work.

1. Does the writing give facts about the hero and tell what lesson can be learned from the hero's actions?

Me: 1 2 3 4 5
Partner: 1 2 3 4 5

2. Does the writing include information from the article?

Me: 1 2 3 4 5
Partner: 1 2 3 4 5

3. Is there at least one Word Bank word used?

Me: 1 2 3 4 5
Partner: 1 2 3 4 5

4. Are grammar, usage, and mechanics correct?

Me: 1 2 3 4 5
Partner: 1 2 3 4 5

Check It and Fix It

After you have written your article, check your work. Imagine you are a newspaper editor checking the article before it is published.

1. Is everything written clearly and correctly? Use the checklist on the right to see.

2. Trade articles with a classmate. Talk over ways you both might improve your articles. Use the ideas to revise your work.

3. For help with grammar, usage, and mechanics, go to the Handbook on pages 189–226.

Vocabulary Workshop

Add these words to your personal word bank by practicing them.

WORD BANK: contribute • inform • react • source • speak

Your Choice

What other new words in the article would you like to remember? List them.

_____

_____

_____

Define It

Complete the chart below. First, write what each Word Bank word means. Then write the context clues from the article that helped you understand the word's meaning. Context clues are words or phrases around the word you do not know. The context clues can give you hints about the word's meaning.

Word COACH

When you are not sure what a word means, look at the other words in the sentence for clues. Look at the sentences before and after the sentence with the word.

Word	Word Meaning	Context Clues from Article
contribute	to give something	Hernandez had to give his help.
inform		
react		
source		
speak		

Show You Know

Write a comic strip in the space below. Use all the Word Bank words in a way that shows you understand their meanings.

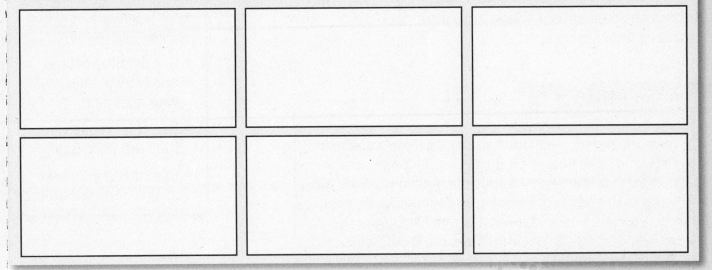

Prefix: *re-*

- Adding the prefix *re-* to a word changes the word's meaning. *Re-* usually means "again" or "back." A rerun, for example, is a program that is being run, or aired, again.

- Complete each sentence by circling the correct word in parentheses.

The newscaster asked the witness to (call, recall) what happened during the tornado. The witness (stated, restated) what she saw. A man walking by a building heard a loud crash. He quickly (reacted, action) when he saw a woman pinned under a fallen roof. When he (viewed, reviewed) his actions later, the man said he saw someone in danger, so he just did what he could to help.

The following words are in the same word family. What are some other words that have *act* in them? Add two to the list.

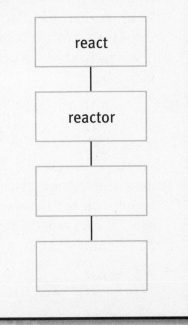

| react |
| reactor |
| |
| |

Write About It!

You have read an article about salaries. Now you will write about the topic. Read the writing prompt. It gives your writing assignment.

WRITING RUBRIC

In your response, you should:

- State your opinion and give reasons for it.
- Use details from the article as the basis of your argument.
- Use at least one word from the Word Bank.
- Use correct grammar, usage, and mechanics.

Writing Prompt

In your opinion, should the size of a person's salary be determined by how much the person helps society or by how entertaining or famous the person is? Write a letter to the editor of a local newspaper. In your letter, give your opinion and support it with ideas from the article. Use at least one word from the Word Bank.

entertain • media • teach • transmit

Prewrite It

Once you are sure you understand the prompt, plan what you want to say.

1. Review your notes from the class discussion. Use the organizer on the right to jot down your thoughts.

2. Reread the article. Look for more reasons that support or explain your opinion. Add those to your organizer.

3. Take another look at your opinion. Do you need to change it in any way after rereading the article? If so, make the changes. Read through all the reasons you listed. Cross out the reasons that are not strong.

My Opinion

> Your opinion is what you think about big salaries.

My Reasons

> Your reasons explain your opinion.

Draft It

Now use your plan to draft, or write, a letter of opinion. The writing frame below will help you.

1. Start by giving your opinion. You have three choices of opinion. Underline your choice.

2. Then give your reasons. Read the second sentence below. Finish the thought by giving strong reasons for your opinion. Make sure you explain your reasons with ideas from the article.

Dear Editor:

I think that celebrities' salaries are (too high, just fine, too low).

I think this because _____

_____

_____

_____

_____

_____

_____

_____

_____

_____

Check It and Fix It

After you have written your letter, check your work. Be sure that it explains your opinion clearly.

1. Is everything written clearly and correctly? Use the checklist on the right to see.

2. Trade your work with a classmate. Talk over ways to improve your letters. Use the ideas to revise your work.

3. For help with grammar, usage, and mechanics, go to the Handbook on pages 189–226.

Writing COACH

If you have trouble putting ideas into words, work with a partner. Tell your partner what you want to say. Ask the person to write it down for you. Use the person's notes to help you write.

✔ **CHECKLIST**

Evaluate your writing. A score of "5" is excellent. A score of "1" means you need to do more work. Then ask a partner to rate your work.

1. **Does the letter give an opinion and support it with reasons?**

   Me: 1 2 3 4 5
   Partner: 1 2 3 4 5

2. **Are there ideas from the article in the letter?**

   Me: 1 2 3 4 5
   Partner: 1 2 3 4 5

3. **Is there at least one Word Bank word used?**

   Me: 1 2 3 4 5
   Partner: 1 2 3 4 5

4. **Are grammar, usage, and mechanics correct?**

   Me: 1 2 3 4 5
   Partner: 1 2 3 4 5

Vocabulary Workshop

Add these words to your personal word bank by practicing them.

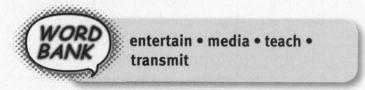

entertain • media • teach • transmit

Define It

Fill in the chart with the Word Bank words. Write what each word means. Then circle the number that tells how well you understand each word. Circle "4" if you understand it completely. Circle "1" if you are not sure you understand the word at all. Use the example as a model.

What It Means	entertain
To entertain is to amuse someone.	**How Well I Understand It** 1 2 3 ④
What It Means	
	How Well I Understand It 1 2 3 4
What It Means	
	How Well I Understand It 1 2 3 4
What It Means	
	How Well I Understand It 1 2 3 4

Show You Know

For each word from the Word Bank, write a clue sentence for a partner to see if he or she can match it with the correct term. Use the clue for the word *entertain* as a model.

• This word describes something that a magician or singer can do.

1. _____

2. _____

3. _____

4. _____

Word Play

Using exact words in your writing can make what you write more lively and detailed. In the chart below, list additional specific words that mean the same or about the same as the Word Bank words. Think of words that give a precise meaning. Examples are shown.

Word Bank Words	Similar Words
entertain	amuse, interest
teach	explain, demonstrate
media	
transmit	

Now try some of the words to see how they can make your writing more precise. Rewrite each of the sentences, substituting one of your words for the boldfaced word.

1. Part of a babysitter's job may be to **entertain** the children.

_____

_____

2. A scientist can **teach** a concept by performing laboratory experiments.

_____

_____

Write About It!

You have read an article about teens and allowances.
Now you will write about the topic. Read the writing
prompt. It gives your writing assignment.

In your response, you should:

- Write a report about teen allowances.
- Use details from the article to support your opinions.
- Use at least one word from the Word Bank.
- Use correct grammar, usage, and mechanics.

Writing Prompt

Imagine that you are a reporter for a TV news program
for teens. Write a short report on allowances. In your
report, write how much allowance you think teens
should get and whether they should be required to
work for it. Use ideas from the article and at least one
word from the Word Bank.

contribute • copy • learn • produce • relate

Prewrite It

Once you are sure you
understand the prompt, plan
what you want to say.

1. Review your notes from
   the class discussion. Begin
   adding details to the
   organizer.

2. After you read the article,
   list more details. Write
   details that support the idea
   of teen allowances as well
   as details that count against
   it. List any details about
   whether teens should have
   to work for allowances.

3. Then write whether teens
   should receive allowances.
   For teens who do receive
   them, write whether the
   teens should have to work for
   them. List reasons for your
   opinions from the article.
   Circle the most convincing
   details in your organizer.

Should teens receive allowances? If yes, how much should they get?	Reasons to Give Teens Allowances
	Reasons Not to Give Teens Allowances
Should teens work for allowances?	Reasons Teens Should Work
	Reasons Teens Should Not Work

Draft It

Now use your plan to write your report. The writing frame below will help you.

1. Start with your opinion about whether teens should get allowances by underlining the appropriate choice in the first statement. Then tell whether teens should work for allowances by underlining a choice in the second statement.

2. Support your opinions with reasons. If you support teen allowances, be sure to mention how much they should get.

In my opinion, teens (should, should not) get allowances.

Teens (should, should not) work for their allowances. I think

this because _____

_____

_____

_____

_____

_____

_____

_____

_____

Check It and Fix It

After you have written your report, check your work. Imagine that you are reading the report for the first time.

1. Is everything written clearly and correctly? Use the checklist on the right to see.

2. Trade your work with a classmate. Talk over ways to improve your reports. Use the ideas to revise your work.

3. For help with grammar, usage, and mechanics, go to the Handbook on pages 189–226.

Before you write a report that shares your opinion, make a list of reasons for your opinion. Then you can easily get at the reasons you want to include.

✔ **CHECKLIST**

Evaluate your writing. A score of "5" is excellent. A score of "1" means you need to do more work. Then ask a partner to rate your work.

1. **Does the writing clearly state opinions and give reasons for them?**

   Me: 1 2 3 4 5
   Partner: 1 2 3 4 5

2. **Does the writing include details from the article to support the opinions?**

   Me: 1 2 3 4 5
   Partner: 1 2 3 4 5

3. **Is there at least one Word Bank word used?**

   Me: 1 2 3 4 5
   Partner: 1 2 3 4 5

4. **Are grammar, usage, and mechanics correct?**

   Me: 1 2 3 4 5
   Partner: 1 2 3 4 5

Vocabulary Workshop

Add these words to your personal word bank by practicing them.

 **WORD BANK** contribute • copy • learn • produce • relate

Your Choice

What other new words in the article would you like to remember? List them.

_____

_____

_____

Define It

Complete the chart below. First, give a real-life example of each word. Then, tell your connection to the word.

Word	Real-Life Example	My Connection to the Word
contribute		
copy		
learn		
produce		
relate		

Show You Know

Write a short, short story (just a paragraph!) using the Word Bank words in the space below. Be sure your sentences show that you understand the meanings of the words.

Once upon a time _____
_____
_____
_____
_____
_____
_____
_____
_____
_____

Partner Up

Ask a partner to read your story. Then ask your partner these questions: Does the story make sense? Does it show that I know the meanings of the words? If your partner answers no to either question, talk over ways to fix the story. Then make the corrections.

It's Academic

Did you notice that the Word Bank words are academic vocabulary? These are words you may use—or hear your teacher use—in your classes. For example, you might **relate** a story in English class or **contribute** to a science project. Choose a word from the Word Bank and write sentences showing how you might use the word in three different classes you are now taking.

1. _____

2. _____

3. _____

UNIT 4 The Music Mix

Write About It!

You have read an article about music and the moods it creates. Now you will write about the topic. Read the writing prompt. It gives your writing assignment.

Writing Prompt

Imagine that you are on the music committee for a school dance. Write a short proposal to your principal. Tell what song should be played to open the dance. Then explain what mood the song communicates and why this mood is right for the dance. Use ideas from the article and at least one word from the Word Bank.

describe • enrich • express • listen • reveal

Prewrite It

Once you are sure you understand the prompt, plan what you want to say.

1. Review your notes from the class discussion. In the organizer, jot down ideas about music and the moods it creates.

2. Reread the article. Look for additional ideas about the link between music and mood setting. Add those ideas to the organizer.

3. Decide what song you want to propose to the principal. Write it in the organizer and include reasons that this music is appropriate.

Ways That Music Creates a Mood	
Music I Would Propose for the Dance	**Why I Would Propose This Music**

Draft It

Now use your plan to draft, or write, your proposal. The writing frame below will help you.

1. Start by writing which music you would propose to begin the school dance.

2. Include the reasons for your choice in your proposal.

Use words that are appropriate for your audience. Since the audience for this proposal is your principal, use formal language and no slang words.

Dear Principal:

To begin our school dance, I suggest that we

listen to _____.

This is good music to begin the dance

because _____

_____

_____

_____

_____

_____

_____

_____

✔ CHECKLIST

Evaluate your writing. A score of "5" is excellent. A score of "1" means you need to do more work. Then ask a partner to rate your work.

1. **Does the proposal name a piece of music and give reasons for the choice?**

   Me: 1 2 3 4 5
   Partner: 1 2 3 4 5

2. **Does the writing include information from the article about how music can create certain moods?**

   Me: 1 2 3 4 5
   Partner: 1 2 3 4 5

3. **Is there at least one Word Bank word used?**

   Me: 1 2 3 4 5
   Partner: 1 2 3 4 5

4. **Are grammar, usage, and mechanics correct?**

   Me: 1 2 3 4 5
   Partner: 1 2 3 4 5

Check It and Fix It

After you have written your proposal, check your work. Read it aloud to a friend to see if it has the right tone to send to your principal.

1. Is everything written clearly and correctly? Use the checklist on the right to see.

2. Trade your work with a classmate. Talk over ways to improve your proposals. Use the ideas to revise your work.

3. For help with grammar, usage, and mechanics, go to the Handbook on pages 189–226.

Vocabulary Workshop

Add these words to your personal word bank by practicing them.

WORD BANK describe • enrich • express • listen • reveal

Your Choice

What other new words in the article would you like to remember? List them.

_____

_____

_____

Define It

Fill in the chart. In the center oval, write two or three subjects you could write about using the five Word Bank words. Use the example as a model.

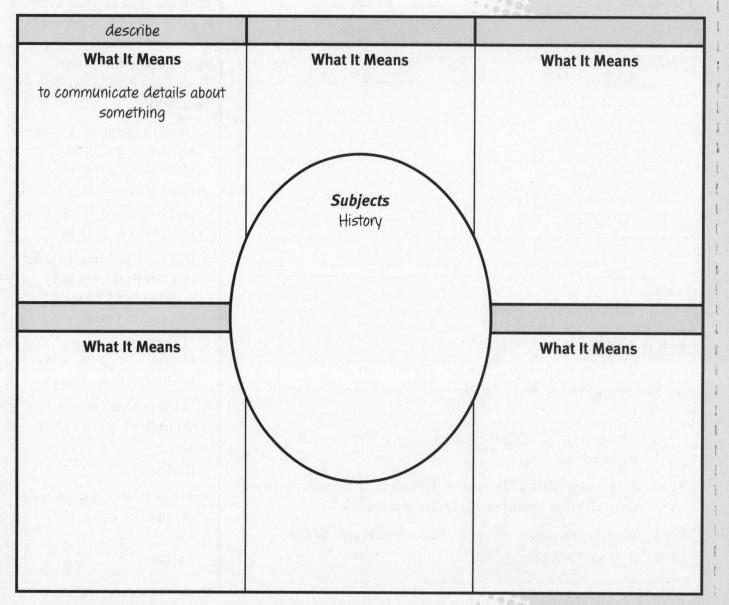

describe		
What It Means	**What It Means**	**What It Means**
to communicate details about something		

Subjects
History

What It Means

What It Means

Show You Know

Write a dialogue, or a conversation between people, in the space below. In your conversation, use all the Word Bank words in a way that shows you understand their meaning.

_____ : _____

_____

_____ : _____

_____

_____ : _____

_____

_____ : _____

_____

Root Words: *scrib, script*

- Many words that have the root *scrib* or *script* have to do with writing. A script, for example, is the written text of what an actor or actors say in a show or play. To describe something means to communicate details about it. You could write a description.

- Complete the paragraph by writing the correct word in each blank.

describe • prescription • scribble

What is the _____ for a better mood? Sometimes it is music! _____ the titles of a few of your favorite songs. Close your eyes and imagine you are listening to them. What feelings can you _____? Do you feel better yet?

The words below belong to the same word family. Highlight the suffix in each word. For an extra challenge, tell each word's part or parts of speech.

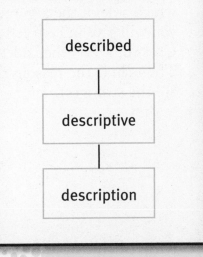

described

descriptive

description

UNIT 4 Follow Your Star

Write About It!

You have read an article about ways in which people act like their favorite celebrities. Now you will write about the topic. Read the writing prompt. It gives your writing assignment.

Writing Prompt

Write an advice column letter telling teens whether you think it is good for them to model themselves after celebrities. Explain your opinion. Use ideas from the article and at least one word from the Word Bank.

media • method • paraphrase • react • technology

Prewrite It

Once you are sure you understand the prompt, plan what you want to write.

1. Review your notes from the class discussion. Begin to fill in the organizer with good and bad reasons to imitate a celebrity.

2. Reread the article. Look for details that you can add to the organizer.

3. Look at both columns of your organizer. Decide which side of the argument you will give in your letter. Cross out the other side. Then circle the reasons that are the strongest.

Should teens copy celebrities?	
Good Reasons	**Bad Reasons**

Draft It

Now use your plan to draft, or write, your letter. The writing frame below will help you.

1. Start by giving your advice. Underline the choice that expresses your opinion about acting like celebrities.

2. The rest of the letter should support your opinion. Include details from the article that support it.

Dear reader:

My advice is that you (should, should not) act like celebrities.

Here are my reasons: _____

_____

_____

_____

_____

_____

_____

_____

_____

_____

Check It and Fix It

After you have written your letter, check your work. Be sure that your writing clearly supports your opinion about whether people should copy celebrities.

1. Is everything written clearly and correctly? Use the checklist on the right to see.

2. Trade letters with a classmate. Talk over ways to improve your letters. Use the ideas to revise your work.

3. For help with grammar, usage, and mechanics, go to the Handbook on pages 189–226.

Writing COACH

Use transitions in your writing, such as *first, more importantly,* and *finally.* Transitions are signals to readers that you are moving from one idea to the next.

✔ **CHECKLIST**

Evaluate your writing. A score of "5" is excellent. A score of "1" means you need to do more work. Then ask a partner to rate your work.

1. **Does the letter give a clearly supported opinion?**

   Me: 1 2 3 4 5
   Partner: 1 2 3 4 5

2. **Does the writing include information from the article?**

   Me: 1 2 3 4 5
   Partner: 1 2 3 4 5

3. **Is there at least one Word Bank word used?**

   Me: 1 2 3 4 5
   Partner: 1 2 3 4 5

4. **Are grammar, usage, and mechanics correct?**

   Me: 1 2 3 4 5
   Partner: 1 2 3 4 5

Vocabulary Workshop

Add these words to your personal word bank by practicing them.

 **media • method • paraphrase • react • technology**

Your Choice

What other new words in the article would you like to remember? List them.

_____

_____

_____

Fill in the chart with the Word Bank words. Write what each word means. Then circle the number that tells how well you understand each word. Circle "4" if you understand it completely. Circle "1" if you are not sure you understand the word at all. Use the example as a model.

What It Means	media
	How Well I Understand It 1 2 3 4
What It Means	
	How Well I Understand It 1 2 3 4
What It Means	
	How Well I Understand It 1 2 3 4
What It Means	
	How Well I Understand It 1 2 3 4
What It Means	
	How Well I Understand It 1 2 3 4

Show You Know

Answer the questions below to show you know how each boldface Word Bank word is used.

1. What parts of the **media** do you think have the most influence on you?

_____

2. What is the best way to learn a **method** for doing something that you have never done before?

_____

3. If you were telling a friend about a movie you had just seen, would you **paraphrase**? Explain why or why not.

_____

4. Name something to which you strongly **react**. Why is your reaction so strong?

_____

5. What is a form of **technology** you know how to use that your grandparents probably did not use at your age?

_____

Word Parts: -logy

- Many words containing -logy relate to the meaning "science" or "study." *Technology* means "the skillful use of science to solve real-life problems" or "devices developed through the use of science." *Biology* means "the science or study of life-forms."

- Combine each of the following roots with -logy to write a new word next to the word's meaning.

Roots

geo: "earth" **morph:** "form or structure"
cardio: "heart" **graph:** "writing"

1. The study of handwriting: _____

2. The study of the earth: _____

3. The study of the heart: _____

4. The study of the form or structure of life-forms: _____

Use suffixes with the word *technology* to create two other words in the same word family.

```
┌──────────────┐
│  technology  │
└──────────────┘
       │
┌──────────────┐
│              │
└──────────────┘
       │
┌──────────────┐
│              │
└──────────────┘
```

Write About It!

You have read an article about aging athletes. Now you will write about the topic. Read the writing prompt. It gives your writing assignment.

Writing Prompt

Imagine that you have been invited to take part in a debate. Your debate question is this: Should talented older athletes retire to make room for younger athletes, or should older athletes keep playing? Write a short speech telling what you think and why. Use ideas from the article and at least one word from the Word Bank.

argue • inform • learn • speak • teach

WRITING RUBRIC

In your response, you should:

- State a viewpoint about aging athletes.

- Use details from the article for support.

- Use at least one word from the Word Bank.

- Use correct grammar, usage, and mechanics.

Prewrite It

Once you are sure you understand the prompt, plan what you want to say.

1. Review your notes from the class discussion. Begin to list your ideas in the organizer.

2. Reread the article. Look for more details to add to your organizer.

3. Look back at your organizer to see which details are strongest. Circle the details you want to be sure to include.

My Opinion

_____

_____

Details That Support My Opinion

_____

_____

_____

_____

_____

_____

_____

Draft It

Now use your plan to draft, or write, your speech. The writing frame below will help you.

1. Start with your opinion. Underline the choice that best completes your thoughts.

2. In your response, include details from the article to support your opinion.

If you have trouble putting your ideas into words, work with a partner. As you write, read aloud and ask your partner if the language sounds right.

In my opinion, older athletes should (retire, keep on playing).

My reasons for this opinion are _____

_____

_____

_____

_____

_____

_____

_____

_____

_____

_____

_____

✔ CHECKLIST

Evaluate your writing. A score of "5" is excellent. A score of "1" means you need to do more work. Then ask a partner to rate your work.

1. **Does the speech clearly state an opinion?**

   Me: 1 2 3 4 5
   Partner: 1 2 3 4 5

2. **Does the speech include supporting details from the article?**

   Me: 1 2 3 4 5
   Partner: 1 2 3 4 5

3. **Is there at least one Word Bank word used?**

   Me: 1 2 3 4 5
   Partner: 1 2 3 4 5

4. **Are grammar, usage, and mechanics correct?**

   Me: 1 2 3 4 5
   Partner: 1 2 3 4 5

Check It and Fix It

After you have written your speech, check your work. Imagine that you are listening to the words as a speech. Does the speech make sense?

1. Is everything written clearly and correctly? Use the checklist on the right to see.

2. Trade speeches with a classmate. Talk over ways to improve your speeches. Use the ideas to revise your work.

3. For help with grammar, usage, and mechanics, go to the Handbook on pages 189–226.

Vocabulary Workshop

Add these words to your personal word bank by practicing them.

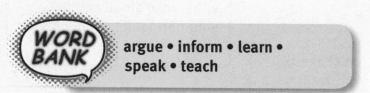

WORD BANK   argue • inform • learn • speak • teach

Your Choice

What other new words in the article would you like to remember? List them.

_____

_____

_____

Define It

Choose two words from the Word Bank and write them in the small boxes below. In the "Connection" box, describe how the two words are connected. Do this for three sets of words. One word will be used twice.

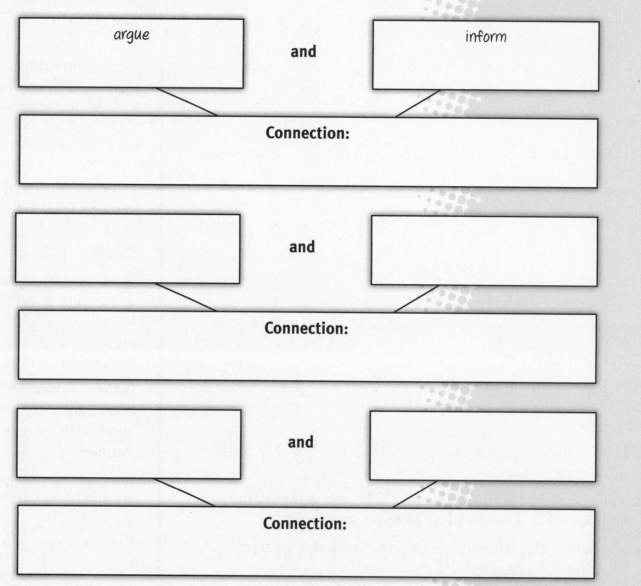

argue	and	inform

Connection:

	and	

Connection:

	and	

Connection:

Show You Know

To show that you understand the words from the Word Bank, write three sentences. In each sentence, use and highlight two of the Word Bank words. You will use one word twice.

1. _____

   _____

2. _____

   _____

3. _____

   _____

Partner Up

Read your partner the sentences you wrote with words left out. Can your partner figure out what words go in the "blanks"? If not, you might need to rewrite to make clearer sentences.

Context Clues

- Sometimes, you can figure out what an unfamiliar word means by using context clues. The context of a word is the setting in which the word appears. It includes words and ideas around the word.

- Circle context clues that tell you what each underlined word means. Then use the clues to write a definition for the word.

1. Older athletes are still a <u>novelty</u>, but advancements in sports medicine have opened up new possibilities.

   _____

2. Add the lessons that older athletes have learned through years of playing their sport. You get <u>well-rounded</u> athletes who can make good decisions as they compete.

   _____

3. Although aging athletes can take care of their bodies, their abilities still <u>decline</u>.

   _____

Writing Reflection

What is the best way to communicate?

Look through your writing from this unit and choose the best piece.
Reflect on this piece of writing by completing each sentence below.

My best piece of writing from this unit is _____

_____

I chose this piece because _____

_____

_____

While I was writing, one goal I had was _____

_____

I accomplished this goal by _____

_____

_____

This writing helped me think more about the Big Question because

_____

_____

One thing I learned while writing that can help me in the future is

_____

_____

UNIT 5

Do others see us more clearly than we see ourselves?

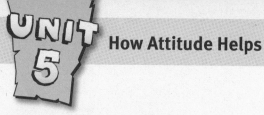

Write About It!

You have read an article about how important attitude is in being successful. Now you will write about the topic. Read the writing prompt. It gives your writing assignment.

Writing Prompt

Do you consider yourself a mostly positive or negative person? Write a diary entry describing yourself. Explain if you think negative thoughts can keep you down and why. Use ideas from the article and at least one word from the Word Bank.

characteristic • focus • perception • reflect • setting

WRITING RUBRIC

In your response, you should:

- Write a diary entry explaining if you are positive or negative.

- Give reasons based on the article you read.

- Use at least one word from the Word Bank.

- Use correct grammar, usage, and mechanics.

Prewrite It

Once you are sure you understand the prompt, plan what you want to say.

1. Review your notes from the class discussion. Do you usually have a positive or negative attitude? Why? Jot down your thoughts in the organizer on the right.

2. Reread the article. Look for additional reasons that support or explain your thoughts. Add those to your organizer.

3. Take another look at your notes. Do you need to change them in any way after rereading the article? If so, make the changes. Look for notes that go together as a way to prepare to write your diary entry.

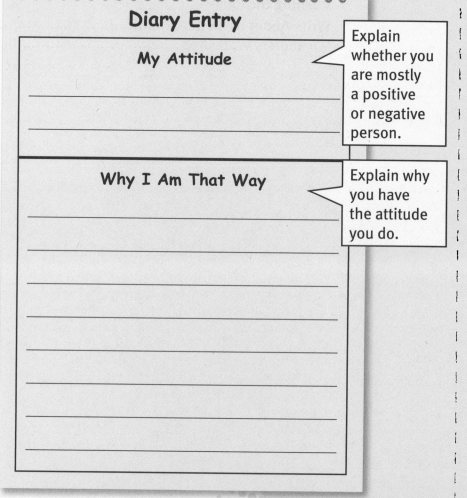

Diary Entry

My Attitude

Explain whether you are mostly a positive or negative person.

Why I Am That Way

Explain why you have the attitude you do.

Draft It

Now use your plan to draft, or write, a diary entry. The writing frame below will help you.

1. Start by describing your attitude. There are three possible ways to describe your attitude. Underline your choice.

2. Then write the reasons you think you have this type of attitude. Be sure to address negative thoughts and how you think they might affect your attitude. Make sure to explain your reasons with ideas from the article.

Writing COACH

If you have trouble organizing your thoughts, work with a partner. Tell your partner what you want to say in your diary entry. Have your partner write the ideas down in outline form. Use your partner's outline to write.

Dear Diary,

In general, I feel I have a (positive, negative, mixed) attitude

toward most things. The reason I feel this way is _____

_____

_____

_____

_____

_____

_____

_____

_____

✔ CHECKLIST

Evaluate your writing. A score of "5" is excellent. A score of "1" means you need to do more work. Then ask a partner to rate your work.

1. **Does the diary entry describe an attitude clearly?**

   Me: 1 2 3 4 5
   Partner: 1 2 3 4 5

2. **Are there ideas from the article?**

   Me: 1 2 3 4 5
   Partner: 1 2 3 4 5

3. **Is there at least one Word Bank word used?**

   Me: 1 2 3 4 5
   Partner: 1 2 3 4 5

4. **Are grammar, usage, and mechanics correct?**

   Me: 1 2 3 4 5
   Partner: 1 2 3 4 5

Check It and Fix It

After you have written your diary entry, check your work. Try to imagine that you have never read the text before.

1. Is everything written clearly and correctly? Use the checklist on the right to see.

2. Trade your work with a classmate. Talk over ways to improve your diary entries. Use the ideas to revise your work.

3. For help with grammar, usage, and mechanics, go to the Handbook on pages 189–226.

Vocabulary Workshop

Add these words to your personal word bank by practicing them.

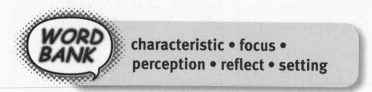

WORD BANK

characteristic • focus • perception • reflect • setting

Define It

Choose two words from the Word Bank and write them in the small boxes below. In the "Connection" box, describe how the two words are connected. Do this for three sets of words. You will have to use one word twice.

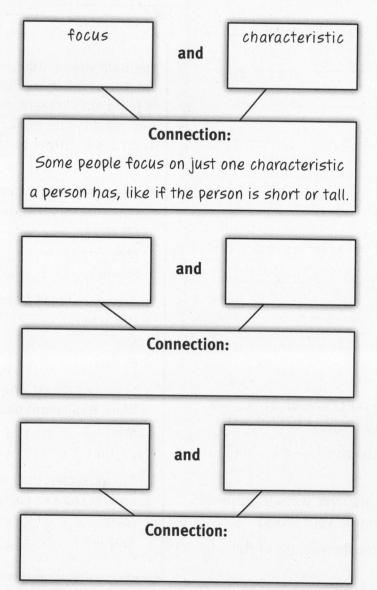

focus **and** characteristic

Connection:
Some people focus on just one characteristic a person has, like if the person is short or tall.

and

Connection:

and

Connection:

Your Choice

What other new words in the article would you like to remember? List them.

_____

_____

_____

Word COACH

A good way to remember new words is to use them soon after learning them. Try to use one of your new words the next time you talk to someone.

Show You Know

Answer the questions below to show you know what each boldface Word Bank word means.

1. What does it mean if an action you take **reflects** a belief or an idea you have?

   _____

   _____

2. Give an example of when you had to **focus** to complete a job.

   _____

   _____

3. The **setting** of a story describes what part of the story?

   _____

   _____

4. How does a **characteristic** give us information about someone?

   _____

   _____

5. If your **perception** of a situation is right, that means you did what?

   _____

   _____

Partner Up

Trade your answers with a partner. Check each other's answers to see if they are correct. If some are not, discuss how to better remember what the words mean in the future.

It's Academic

Did you notice that some of the Word Bank words are academic vocabulary? These are words you might hear a teacher use in class. For example, you might study the **setting** of a play in a literature class or discuss the **setting** of a picture for a photography class. Choose three words from the Word Bank. Write sentences showing how you might use the words in a class you are taking. For a challenge, try to use the same word to show how it applies to two different classes.

1. _____

2. _____

3. _____

Write About It!

You have read an article about happiness. Now you will write about the topic. Read the writing prompt. It gives your writing assignment.

WRITING RUBRIC

In your response, you should:

- Write a plan for a new reality show.

- Use facts and information from the article you read.

- Use at least one word from the Word Bank.

- Use correct grammar, usage, and mechanics.

Writing Prompt

Imagine you are a writer for a new teen reality show called "Happiness Is." Write a treatment, or plan, for the first episode of the show. Tell what activities teens on the show could participate in. Then explain why these activities make teens happy. Use ideas from the article and at least one word from the Word Bank.

appreciate • complete • define • ignore • reaction

Prewrite It

Once you are sure you understand the prompt, plan what you want to say.

1. Review your notes from the class discussion. What kinds of activities make teens happy? Jot down any ideas in the web on the right. Then write down reasons why you think teens like these activities.

2. Reread the article and look for more information you can use in your episode treatment.

3. Take another look at your web. Do you need to change it in any way after rereading the article? If so, make the changes.

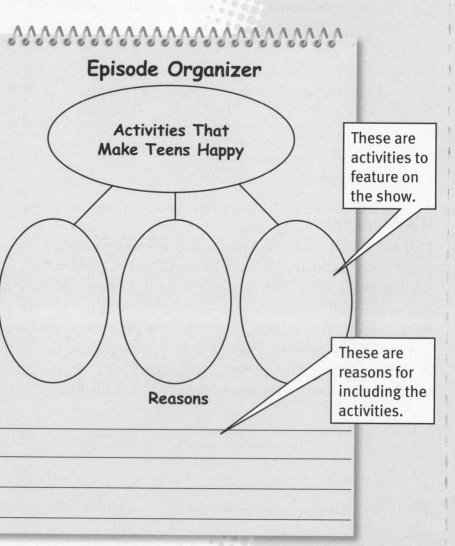

Episode Organizer

Activities That Make Teens Happy

These are activities to feature on the show.

Reasons

These are reasons for including the activities.

Draft It

Now use your plan to draft, or write, your show treatment. The writing frame below will help you.

1. Start by making a statement about the general concept of the show. Be creative. Use the opening line below to begin your treatment.

2. Then list three activities you have decided to use. Describe the activities, and then give your reasons why the activities make teens happy. Make sure to use facts from the article.

"Happiness Is" Teen Reality Show Episode

"Happiness Is," a new teen reality show, will

_____

_____

_____

_____ .

Activity 1: _____

_____

Activity 2: _____

_____

Activity 3: _____

_____

Check It and Fix It

After you have written your treatment, check your work. Imagine that you have never read the treatment before.

1. Is everything written clearly and correctly? Use the checklist on the right to see.

2. Exchange work with a classmate. Talk over ways you both might improve your treatments. Use the ideas to revise your work.

3. For help with grammar, usage, and mechanics, go to the Handbook on pages 189–226.

Writing COACH

If you have trouble putting ideas into words, work with a partner. Explain to your partner what you want to say. Have your partner repeat your idea back to you in his or her own words. Then write down the idea based on what you and your partner both said.

✔ **CHECKLIST**

Evaluate your writing. A score of "5" is excellent. A score of "1" means you need to do more work. Then ask a partner to rate your work.

1. **Does the plan explain the activities and reasons clearly?**

   Me: 1 2 3 4 5
   Partner: 1 2 3 4 5

2. **Are there facts from the article that support the plan?**

   Me: 1 2 3 4 5
   Partner: 1 2 3 4 5

3. **Is there at least one Word Bank word used?**

   Me: 1 2 3 4 5
   Partner: 1 2 3 4 5

4. **Are grammar, usage, and mechanics correct?**

   Me: 1 2 3 4 5
   Partner: 1 2 3 4 5

Vocabulary Workshop

Add these words to your personal word bank by practicing them.

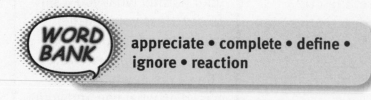

appreciate • complete • define • ignore • reaction

Your Choice

What other new words in the article would you like to remember? List them.

_____

_____

_____

Define It

In each of the boxes below, write words from the Word Bank you might use when writing about each subject. You can put individual words in as many as all three boxes if it is appropriate.

Thinking

Talking

reaction

Feeling

Show You Know

Write a comic strip in the space below. Use all the Word Bank words in a way that shows you understand their meanings.

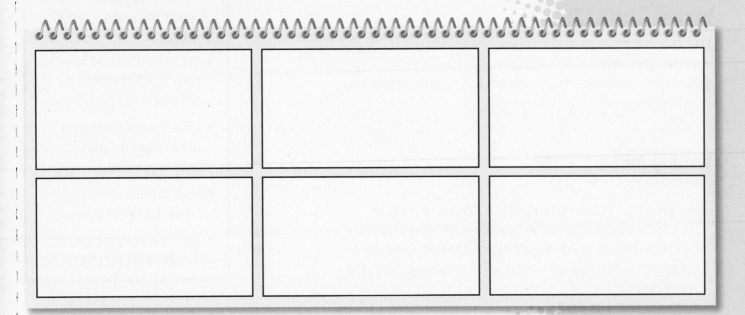

Context Clues

- Sometimes, you can figure out what an unfamiliar word means by using context clues. The context of a word is the sentence in which the word appears and sometimes other nearby sentences.

- Circle context clues that tell you what each underlined word means. Then use the clues to write a definition for the word.

1. They might have extra money or time to share, or their <u>appreciation</u> for others' kindnesses makes them want to give back.

---

2. Your eyes are glued to the television set. You cannot <u>ignore</u> watching a family in need receiving a brand new house.

These words are part of the same word family. What are some other words that have the word *react* in them? Add one to the list.

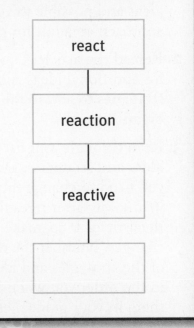

react

reaction

reactive

Write About It!

You have read an article about how difficult it can be to help friends admit to having hurtful behavior. Now you will write about the topic. Read the writing prompt. It gives your writing assignment.

In your response, you should:

- Write guidelines for how to help a friend with serious problems.

- Give reasons for your ideas based on the article you read.

- Use at least one word from the Word Bank.

- Use correct grammar, usage, and mechanics.

Writing Prompt

Imagine that you need to get the advice or help of an adult to help a friend in trouble. Use information from the article to write guidelines that you and your classmates can follow. Use at least one word from the Word Bank.

appearance • consider • image • perspective • reveal

Prewrite It

Once you are sure you understand the prompt, plan what you want to say.

1. Review your notes from the class discussion. How can you help a friend deal with problems? In the organizer on the right, jot down your ideas and possible ways to approach an adult for help.

2. Reread the article. Look for additional ideas and strategies to add to the organizer.

3. Read through your list of ideas and strategies. Do you need to change them in any way after rereading the article? If so, make the changes. Number the rest of the strategies and ideas in the order you will use them in your guidelines.

Guidelines for Helping a Friend in Trouble

Ways to Help	Ways to Get an Adult to Help

Draft It

Now use your plan to draft, or write, your guidelines. The writing frame below will help you.

1. Start by explaining the purpose of the guidelines. The guidelines should show how teens could get an adult involved to help a friend. Use the first line to get started.

2. Then list the steps you would take. List them starting with the most important at the top. Make sure to use ideas from the article in your guidelines.

Exchange your guidelines with a partner and read through them. Look for any language that is not clear. Work together to think of ways to clarify any of the guidelines that might be confusing.

Guidelines for Helping a Friend in Trouble

The purpose of these guidelines is to _____

_____

_____

_____

Step 1: _____

_____

_____

_____

_____

CHECKLIST

Evaluate your writing. A score of "5" is excellent. A score of "1" means you need to do more work. Then ask a partner to rate your work.

1. **Do the guidelines state clear steps and strategies?**

   Me: 1 2 3 4 5
   Partner: 1 2 3 4 5

2. **Are there ideas from the article used in the guidelines?**

   Me: 1 2 3 4 5
   Partner: 1 2 3 4 5

3. **Is there at least one Word Bank word used?**

   Me: 1 2 3 4 5
   Partner: 1 2 3 4 5

4. **Are grammar, usage, and mechanics correct?**

   Me: 1 2 3 4 5
   Partner: 1 2 3 4 5

Check It and Fix It

After you have written your guidelines, check your work. Try to read them with a "fresh eye." Imagine that you have never read the guidelines before.

1. Is everything written clearly and correctly? Use the checklist on the right to see.

2. Trade your work with a classmate. Talk over ways you both might improve your guidelines. Use the ideas to revise your work.

3. For help with grammar, usage, and mechanics, go to the Handbook on pages 189–226.

Vocabulary Workshop

Add these words to your personal word bank by practicing them.

 appearance • consider • image • perspective • reveal

Your Choice

What other new words in the article would you like to remember? List them.

_____

_____

_____

Define It

Fill in the chart with the Word Bank words. Tell what each word means. Then circle the number that tells how well you understand each word. Circle "4" if you understand it completely. Circle "1" if you are not sure you understand the word at all. Use the example as a model.

What It Means	appearance
the way someone or something looks	**How Well I Understand It** 1 2 3 ④
What It Means	
	How Well I Understand It 1 2 3 4
What It Means	
	How Well I Understand It 1 2 3 4
What It Means	
	How Well I Understand It 1 2 3 4
What It Means	
	How Well I Understand It 1 2 3 4

Show You Know

To show that you understand the Word Bank words, write a clue for each word. Exchange clues with a partner. See whether your partner can identify the correct word for each clue. Use the clue for the word *reveal* as a model.

- If you let people know something that was a secret, you do this.

1. _____

2. _____

3. _____

4. _____

5. _____

Partner Up

Trade your sentences with a partner and try to answer them. Check each other's answers to see if they are correct. If you or your partner got any wrong, figure out if any clues could be more clearly written.

Word Endings: *-ance, -ence*

- The suffix *-ance* or *-ence* means "the state of" or "condition." When you add *-ance* or *-ence* to a verb or adjective, it changes the word to a noun.

  Verb: I would love to **appear** in a movie someday.

  Noun: I would love to make an **appearance** in a play.

- Read the paragraph below. For each set of words in parentheses, circle the word that makes the most sense in the sentence. Use your knowledge of word parts to help you.

   We have a clear (differ, difference, different) of opinion about this. I think the actor's (perform, performing, performance) was great. I know his voice was (annoyance, annoying), and I usually don't like movies with so much (violence, violent). But I still think his acting was truly (brilliance, brilliant).

UNIT 5 Pushing Buttons

Write About It!

You have read an article about gossip. Now you will write about the topic. Read the writing prompt. It gives your writing assignment.

Writing Prompt

Do you think cyberbullies should be banned from the Internet? Or is it important to protect free speech? Write a letter to your state representative telling what you think and why. Use ideas from the article and at least one word from the Word Bank.

appreciate • assumption • bias • identify • reaction

Prewrite It

Once you are sure you understand the prompt, plan what you want to say.

1. Review your notes from the class discussion. Should cyberbullies be stopped from posting messages? Or do they have the same free speech rights as everyone else? Use the organizer on the right to prepare to write your letter.

2. Reread the article. Look for additional ideas to support your opinion. Add those to your organizer.

3. Take another look at your organizer. Do any of the ideas you have written seem to go together? If so, group similar ideas to help organize your thoughts. Cross out ideas that are repetitive or are not as important as others.

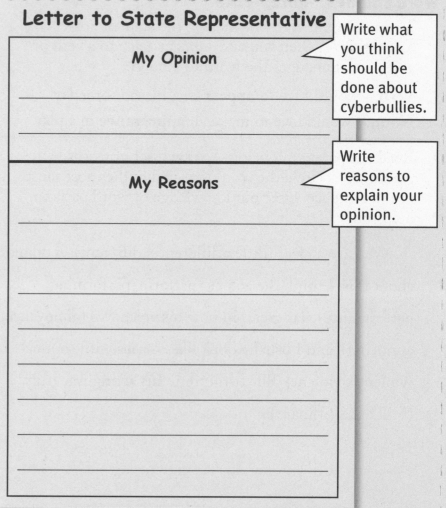

Letter to State Representative

My Opinion

Write what you think should be done about cyberbullies.

My Reasons

Write reasons to explain your opinion.

Draft It

Now use your plan to draft, or write, your letter. The writing frame below will help you.

1. Start by stating your opinion about what you think should be done about cyberbullies. You have two choices of opinion. Underline your opinion.

2. Then give your reasons. Read the second sentence below. Finish the thought by giving strong reasons for your opinion. Make sure you explain your reasons with ideas from the article.

Read a sentence you wrote to your partner. See what your partner understood from the sentence. This can help you decide if your writing needs to be clearer.

Dear State Representative:

Cyberbullies are becoming a big Internet problem. I think the

government (should, should not) get involved to stop them.

I feel this way because _____

_____

_____

_____

_____

_____

_____

_____

✔ CHECKLIST

Evaluate your writing. A score of "5" is excellent. A score of "1" means you need to do more work. Then ask a partner to rate your work.

1. **Does the letter clearly present an opinion?**

   Me: 1 2 3 4 5
   Partner: 1 2 3 4 5

2. **Are there ideas from the article that support the opinion?**

   Me: 1 2 3 4 5
   Partner: 1 2 3 4 5

3. **Is there at least one Word Bank word used?**

   Me: 1 2 3 4 5
   Partner: 1 2 3 4 5

4. **Are grammar, usage, and mechanics correct?**

   Me: 1 2 3 4 5
   Partner: 1 2 3 4 5

Check It and Fix It

After you have written your letter, check your work. Imagine that you have never read the letter before.

1. Is everything written clearly and correctly? Use the checklist on the right to see.

2. Exchange work with a classmate. Talk over ways you both might improve your letters. Use the ideas to revise your work.

3. For help with grammar, usage, and mechanics, go to the Handbook on pages 189–226.

Vocabulary Workshop

Add these words to your personal word bank by practicing them.

 **WORD BANK** appreciate • assumption • bias • identify • reaction

Your Choice

What other new words in the article would you like to remember? List them.

_____

_____

_____

Define It

Complete the chart below. First, tell what the word means. Then, tell what the word does not mean. Use the example as a guide.

Word	What It Is	What It Is Not
appreciate	to value something	not recognizing how important something is
assumption		
bias		
identify		
reaction		

Show You Know

To show that you understand the Word Bank words, write three sentences. In each sentence, use and highlight two of the words. You will use one word twice. Use the example as a model.

- An assumption someone makes can reveal a personal bias.

1. _____

   _____

2. _____

   _____

3. _____

   _____

Multiple-Meaning Words

- When you use a dictionary to find the meaning of a word, you often find more than one definition for the word. Which is the right one? Look at how the word is used in the context of a sentence. For example, which definition for *bias* makes sense below?

  My sewing teacher said to cut the cloth on the <u>bias</u>.

  bias: (a) a like or dislike for something based on its characteristics; (b) slanting line cut across a piece of cloth

  If you chose definition (b), you are right. That definition makes sense in the sentence.

- For each of the sentences below, circle the correct definition of the boldface word.

1. That is quite an **assumption** to make with so little information.

   assumption: (a) taking for granted or supposing;

   (b) taking over another's debts or obligations

2. I would not **identify** myself with that organization.

   identify: (a) recognizing or describing something;

   (b) associating yourself with a group or person

Add suffixes to the word *identify* to create two other words in the same word family.

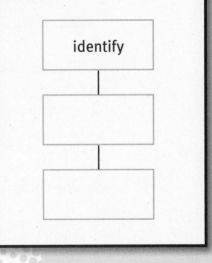

identify

UNIT 5 WRAP UP

Writing Reflection

Do others see us more clearly than we see ourselves?

Look through your writing from this unit and choose the best piece. Reflect on this piece of writing by completing each sentence below.

My best piece of writing from this unit is _____

_____

I chose this piece because _____

_____

_____

While I was writing, one goal I had was _____

_____

I accomplished this goal by _____

_____

_____

This writing helped me think more about the Big Question because

_____

_____

One thing I learned while writing that can help me in the future is

_____

_____

UNIT 6

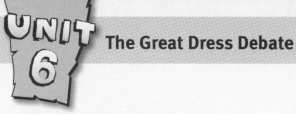

Write About It!

You have read an article about dress codes. Now you will write about the topic. Read the writing prompt. It gives your writing assignment.

Writing Prompt

Imagine your school is having a meeting about creating a dress code. As a student representative, you have been asked to write an agenda for the meeting. On the agenda, list the issues that people at the meeting should talk about. Use ideas from the article and at least one word from the Word Bank.

culture • diversity • environment • individual

Prewrite It

Once you are sure you understand the prompt, plan what you want to say.

1. Review your notes from the class discussion. If any of your notes are unclear, ask a classmate for help.

2. Reread the article. Look for important issues about school safety and individual freedom. Make notes on the organizer at the right.

3. Take another look at all the points you have listed. Decide what is most important to put on the agenda.

WRITING RUBRIC

In your response, you should:

- Write an agenda for a dress codes meeting.
- Use information from the article to create your points.
- Use at least one word from the Word Bank.
- Use correct grammar, usage, and mechanics.

Dress Code Agenda

Safety Issues	Freedom Issues

Make notes about school safety issues.

Make notes about freedom of expression issues.

Draft It

Now use your plan to draft, or write, an agenda for a meeting about a school dress code. The writing frame below will help you.

1. Write the issues that you think should be discussed in a meeting about dress codes. Begin with the issue you think is most important. Then list other issues that should be discussed.

2. Try not to leave out any important issues. Make sure you include ideas from the article.

Sometimes it helps to talk through what you are going to write. Tell a partner what points you are going to put on your agenda. Discuss whether these are the most important points.

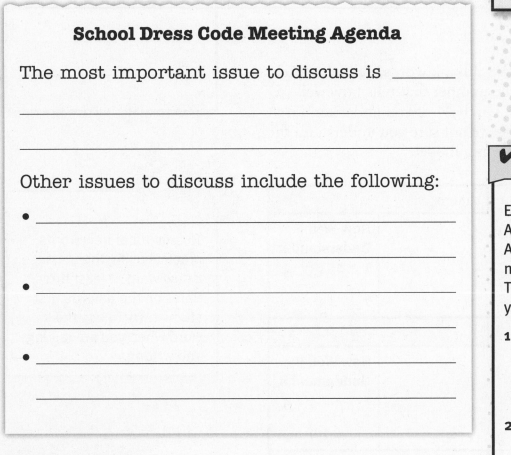

School Dress Code Meeting Agenda

The most important issue to discuss is _____

_____

_____

Other issues to discuss include the following:

- _____

  _____

- _____

  _____

- _____

  _____

Check It and Fix It

After you have written your agenda, check your work. Imagine that you are at the meeting and seeing it for the first time.

1. Is your agenda written clearly and correctly? The checklist on the right will help you find out.

2. Trade your work with a classmate. Talk about ways you both might improve your agendas. Use the ideas to revise your work.

3. For help with grammar, usage, and mechanics, go to the Handbook on pages 189–226.

✔ CHECKLIST

Evaluate your writing. A score of "5" is excellent. A score of "1" means you need to do more work. Then ask a partner to rate your work.

1. **Does the agenda state the issues clearly?**

   Me: 1 2 3 4 5
   Partner: 1 2 3 4 5

2. **Are ideas from the article used in the agenda?**

   Me: 1 2 3 4 5
   Partner: 1 2 3 4 5

3. **Is there at least one Word Bank word used?**

   Me: 1 2 3 4 5
   Partner: 1 2 3 4 5

4. **Are grammar, usage, and mechanics correct?**

   Me: 1 2 3 4 5
   Partner: 1 2 3 4 5

Vocabulary Workshop

Add these words to your personal word bank by practicing them.

 culture • diversity • environment • individual

Define It

Fill in the chart with the Word Bank words. Tell what each word means. Then circle the number that tells how well you understand each word. Circle "4" if you understand it completely. Circle "1" if you are not sure you understand the word at all. Use the example as a model.

What It Means	culture	
traditions and beliefs that me and my family have	**How Well I Understand It** 1 2 ③ 4	
What It Means		
	How Well I Understand It 1 2 3 4	
What It Means		
	How Well I Understand It 1 2 3 4	
What It Means		
	How Well I Understand It 1 2 3 4	

Your Choice

What other new words in the article would you like to remember? List them.

_____

_____

_____

Word COACH

To remember new words, practice using them. Use a new word at least three times on the day you first study it. Try to use the word when you are talking and writing.

Show You Know

For each word from the Word Bank, write a clue sentence for a partner to see if he or she can match it with the correct term. See the example for the word *culture*.

- This is what people from a particular country or other group have in common.

1. _____

_____

2. _____

_____

3. _____

_____

4. _____

_____

Partner Up

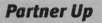

Exchange clue sentences with a partner to read. If you have trouble figuring out any clue sentence, talk with your partner about how to change the sentence.

Word Endings: *-ment*

- A word that has *-ment* as its ending is usually a noun. The rest of the word carries the meaning. The ending of the word *entertainment*, for example, tells you it is a noun. The rest of the word tells you that it means "that which entertains."

- Circle the correct word in each set of parentheses.

1. I could see Kevin's (amaze, amazement) when Brianne walked in.

2. Holidays always bring with them a lot of (merry, merriment).

3. Pioneers liked to (settle, settlement) near rivers.

- Now, write a sentence using a word with the suffix *-ment*.

_____

_____

ALL IN THE FAMILY

These words belong to the same word family. Highlight the suffix on each word. For an extra challenge, tell each word's part of speech.

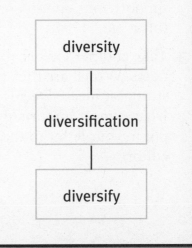

diversity

diversification

diversify

Write About It!

You have read an article about ways science is trying to control weather. Now you will write about the topic. Read the writing prompt. It gives your writing assignment.

Writing Prompt

After reading "Commanding the Weather," do you think people should try to control the weather? Write a letter to the editor of your local newspaper. Explain whether you think a plan to seed clouds during a drought in your area is a good idea. Use ideas from the article and at least one word from the Word Bank.

common • community • duty • team • voice

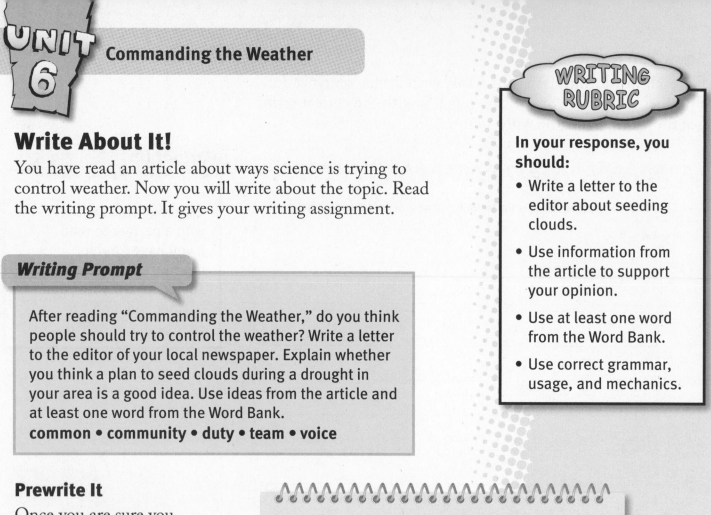

WRITING RUBRIC

In your response, you should:

• Write a letter to the editor about seeding clouds.

• Use information from the article to support your opinion.

• Use at least one word from the Word Bank.

• Use correct grammar, usage, and mechanics.

Prewrite It

Once you are sure you understand the prompt, plan what you want to say.

1. Review your notes from the class discussion. Pay attention to the effects of controlling the weather. Make notes on the organizer at the right.

2. Reread the article. Look for examples and facts that support your opinion on this issue.

3. Take another look at your notes. Which are the strongest ideas? Decide what is most important to put in your letter to the editor.

"To Seed or Not to Seed"

Opinion

This is what you think.

Reason	Reason
1.	3.
2.	4.

These are reasons for your opinion.

Draft It

Now use your plan to draft, or write, your letter. The writing frame below will help you.

1. Start by stating your opinion. You have two choices of opinion. Underline your choice.

2. Then give your reasons. Read the second sentence below. Finish the thought by giving reasons that you noted in your organizer. Make sure to explain your reasons with ideas from the article.

Ask your partner to read your letter aloud as if he or she were reading it from a newspaper. Ask your partner if your message is clear in the letter.

To the Editor:

I think we (should, should not) seed clouds to bring rain to our

area. I think this because _____

_____

_____

_____

_____

_____

_____

_____

_____

Check It and Fix It

After you have written your letter, check your work. Imagine that you have never read the message before.

1. Is your letter clear? Have you written it correctly? The checklist on the right will help you check.

2. Trade your work with a classmate. Read each other's letters and talk about how to improve them. Use the ideas to revise your work.

3. For help with grammar, usage, and mechanics, go to the Handbook on pages 189–226.

✔ CHECKLIST

Evaluate your writing. A score of "5" is excellent. A score of "1" means you need to do more work. Then ask a partner to rate your work.

1. **Does the letter state the opinion clearly and explain it?**

   Me: 1 2 3 4 5
   Partner: 1 2 3 4 5

2. **Are there ideas from the article to support the opinion?**

   Me: 1 2 3 4 5
   Partner: 1 2 3 4 5

3. **Is there at least one Word Bank word used?**

   Me: 1 2 3 4 5
   Partner: 1 2 3 4 5

4. **Are grammar, usage, and mechanics correct?**

   Me: 1 2 3 4 5
   Partner: 1 2 3 4 5

Vocabulary Workshop

Add these words to your personal word bank by practicing them.

 **WORD BANK** **common • community • duty • team • voice**

Your Choice

What other new words in the article would you like to remember? List them.

_____

_____

_____

Define It

Fill in the chart. In the center oval, write two or three subjects you could write about using the five Word Bank words. Use the examples as a model.

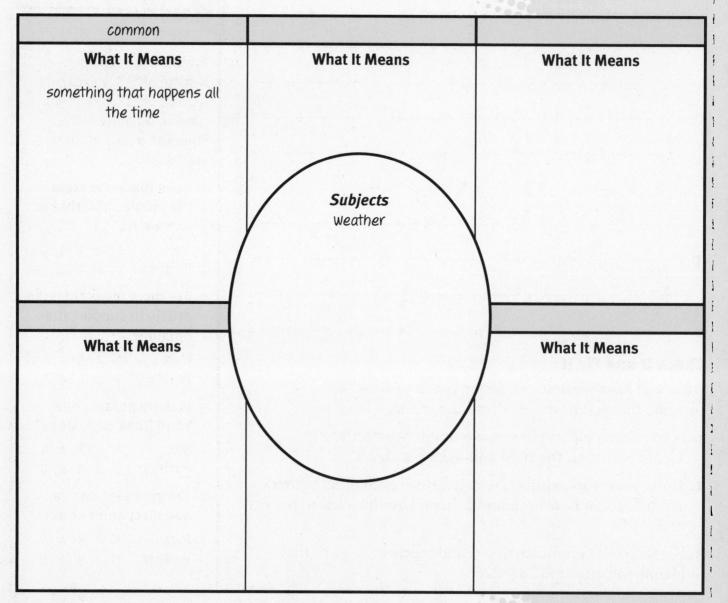

common		
What It Means something that happens all the time	**What It Means**	**What It Means**

Subjects
weather

What It Means

What It Means

Show You Know

Write a short, short story (just a paragraph!) using the Word Bank words. Be sure your sentences show that you understand the meanings of the words.

Once upon a time _____

_____

_____

_____

_____

_____

_____

_____

_____

_____

_____

Partner Up

Ask your partner to read your story. Then ask your partner if the story makes sense. Does it show that you know the meanings of the Word Bank words? If not, your partner can suggest ways to fix the story.

Double-Duty Words

- Some English words can be used as nouns or verbs. The word *voice* is usually used as a noun. It is what you use to speak or sing. As a verb, *voice* means to speak your opinion and have it heard.

- The following sentences are from the article. Look at the boldface word in each one, and then write in the blank whether it is a noun (N) or a verb (V).

1. What if we could **spread** something on the sea to halt a

hurricane? _____

2. Some people **worry** about the consequences of weather

modification. _____

3. The droplets then fall to Earth as **rain**. _____

Write About It!

You have read an article about urban gardens. Now you will write about the topic. Read the writing prompt. It gives your writing assignment.

Writing Prompt

Do you think an urban garden can help a community turn around? Write a proposal to the city council for the use of a vacant lot in your neighborhood. You would read the proposal at a council meeting. Explain what you want to do with the lot and why. Use ideas from the article and at least one word from the Word Bank.

custom • ethnicity • group • unify • various

In your response, you should:

• Write a proposal to the city council for use of a vacant lot.

• Use information from the article in your proposal.

• Use at least one word from the Word Bank.

• Use correct grammar, usage, and mechanics.

Prewrite It

Once you are sure you understand the prompt, plan what you want to say.

1. Look through your notes from the classroom discussion. If you have a question about them, ask a classmate to help you.

2. Reread the article. Make notes about important points on the organizer at the right.

3. Fill out the organizer by using classroom notes and by rereading the article. You do not have to write complete sentences. These notes are for you.

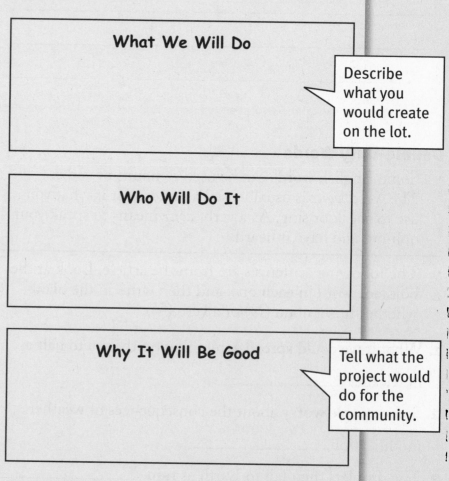

What We Will Do

Describe what you would create on the lot.

Who Will Do It

Why It Will Be Good

Tell what the project would do for the community.

Draft It

Now use your plan to draft, or write, a proposal to the city council. The writing frame below will help you.

1. Start by telling what you want to do with the lot. Use as many details as you can. Then tell who would work on the project and why it would be good for your community.

2. Finish the sentences with ideas you noted in your organizer. Be sure to include ideas from the article you read.

When writing a proposal, keep in mind that your words and sentences should be easy to speak. Ask a partner to read your proposal aloud and listen for any words or sentences that cause him or her problems.

To the City Council:

I am asking for your permission to _____

_____

_____

The people who will work on this project are

_____

_____

_____

We believe this will help the community by

_____

_____

_____

Check It and Fix It

Check your work after you have finished it. Imagine that you are a city council member and are hearing the proposal for the first time.

1. Is your proposal clear? Have you written your ideas correctly? The checklist on the right will help you find out.

2. Trade your work with a classmate. Talk about ways to improve your proposals. Use the ideas to revise your work.

3. For help with grammar, usage, and mechanics, go to the Handbook on pages 189–226.

✔ CHECKLIST

Evaluate your writing. A score of "5" is excellent. A score of "1" means you need to do more work. Then ask a partner to rate your work.

1. **Does the proposal explain clearly what will be done to the lot?**

   Me: 1 2 3 4 5
   Partner: 1 2 3 4 5

2. **Are there good ideas from the article in the proposal?**

   Me: 1 2 3 4 5
   Partner: 1 2 3 4 5

3. **Is there at least one Word Bank word used?**

   Me: 1 2 3 4 5
   Partner: 1 2 3 4 5

4. **Are grammar, usage, and mechanics correct?**

   Me: 1 2 3 4 5
   Partner: 1 2 3 4 5

Vocabulary Workshop

Add these words to your personal word bank by practicing them.

WORD BANK
custom • ethnicity • group • unify • various

Your Choice

What other new words in the article would you like to remember? List them.

_____

_____

_____

Define It

Complete the chart below. Write each Word Bank word, its meaning, and a word it reminds you of. Use the example as a guide.

What It Means	custom
something done on a regular basis	**Word It Reminds Me Of** tradition

What It Means	
	Word It Reminds Me Of _____

What It Means	
	Word It Reminds Me Of _____

What It Means	
	Word It Reminds Me Of _____

What It Means	
	Word It Reminds Me Of _____

Show You Know

To show that you understand the Word Bank words, write three sentences. In each sentence, use and highlight two of the words. You will use one word twice. Use the example as a model.

Partner Up

Trade sentences with a partner. Check each other's sentences to see if the words are used correctly. If a word is used incorrectly, discuss how to revise the sentence. Then make the corrections.

• It is a custom for a group of my relatives to watch the fireworks show on Independence Day.

1. _____

_____

2. _____

_____

3. _____

_____

Word Endings: *-ous*

• The suffix *-ous* can turn a noun into an adjective. Whenever you see *-ous* used in a word, you know that the word means "full of," "having," or "having the qualities of."

• Look at the following definition sentences and fill in the blanks.

1. **Courageous** means "having _____."

2. **Famous** means "having _____."

3. **Joyous** means "full of _____."

4. **Poisonous** means "having the qualities

of _____."

• Choose one of the *-ous* words. Use it in a sentence of your own.

_____

_____

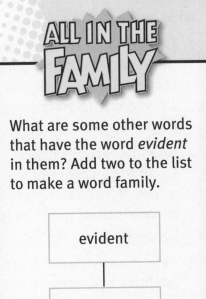

ALL IN THE FAMILY

What are some other words that have the word *evident* in them? Add two to the list to make a word family.

evident

Write About It!

You have read an article about good leaders. Now you will write about the topic. Read the writing prompt. It gives your writing assignment.

Writing Prompt

After reading "What It Takes to Lead," what do you think makes a good leader? Your town is having a "Mayor for a Day" contest for young people. To enter, you need to write a short description of what it takes to be a leader. Use ideas from the article and at least one word from the Word Bank.

duty • individual • team • tradition

Prewrite It

Once you are sure you understand the prompt, plan what you want to say.

1. Look at your notes from the classroom discussion. If they are not clear, talk to a classmate to refresh your memory.

2. Read the article again. Look for qualities of a good leader. Write examples of those kinds of qualities in the web on the right.

3. Take another look at the qualities you have listed. Underneath the web, jot down reasons why it is important for a good leader to have those qualities.

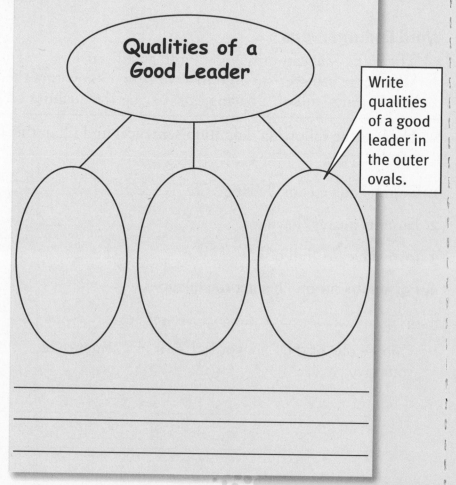

Qualities of a Good Leader

Write qualities of a good leader in the outer ovals.

Draft It

Now use your plan to draft, or write, a short description of a good leader for the contest. The writing frame below will help you.

1. Start by giving your first quality that makes a good leader. Then explain why that quality is important.

2. Then give two more qualities and reasons. Make sure you explain why the qualities are important with ideas from the article.

Talk to a partner about the qualities a leader should have. See what the partner thinks about your choices and discuss them before you write. This could help you explain your reasons more clearly in your writing.

I think a leader should be _____.

This is important because _____

_____

_____.

I also think a leader should be _____.

This is important because _____

_____

_____.

Finally, a leader should be _____.

This is important because _____

_____

_____.

Check It and Fix It

After you have written your description, check your work. Imagine you have never read the description before. Does it makes sense to you?

1. Did you write the description clearly and correctly? The checklist on the right will help you see.

2. Exchange descriptions with a partner. Talk about ways you both might improve your descriptions. Use the ideas to revise your work.

3. For help with grammar, usage, and mechanics, go to the Handbook on pages 189–226.

✔ CHECKLIST

Evaluate your writing. A score of "5" is excellent. A score of "1" means you need to do more work. Then ask a partner to rate your work.

1. **Does the description make the opinions clear?**

   Me: 1 2 3 4 5
   Partner: 1 2 3 4 5

2. **Are there ideas from the article that support the reasons?**

   Me: 1 2 3 4 5
   Partner: 1 2 3 4 5

3. **Is there at least one Word Bank word used?**

   Me: 1 2 3 4 5
   Partner: 1 2 3 4 5

4. **Are grammar, usage, and mechanics correct?**

   Me: 1 2 3 4 5
   Partner: 1 2 3 4 5

Vocabulary Workshop

Add these words to your personal word bank by practicing them.

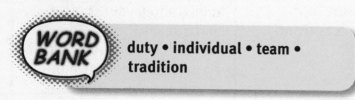

WORD BANK duty • individual • team • tradition

Define It

Choose two words from the Word Bank and write them in the small boxes below. In the "Connection" box, describe how the two words are connected. Do this for two sets of words.

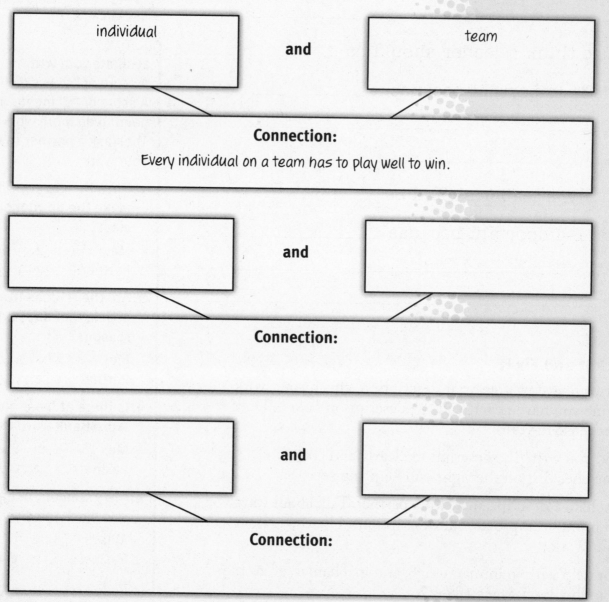

individual

and

team

Connection:
Every individual on a team has to play well to win.

and

Connection:

and

Connection:

Show You Know

Complete the items below to show you know what each boldface Word Bank word means.

1. Describe one thing you think is a **duty** of all people. _____
   _____

2. How is an **individual** different from a group of people? _____
   _____

3. Describe a **team** that you were on or are on now. _____
   _____

4. What is a **tradition** that your family or friends have? _____
   _____

Multiple-Meaning Words

- You will often find more than one definition for a word in a dictionary. Which is the right one? Look at how the word is used in the context of a sentence. For example, which definition for *duty* makes sense below?

  She had to pay a **duty** on the purchases she made on her trip to Paris.

  duty: (a) an action required by a person's job; (b) a tax on imports.

  If you chose definition (b), you are right. That definition makes sense in the sentence.

- Circle the correct meaning for each boldface word in the chart below.

Word in Sentence	Meaning 1	Meaning 2
A **team** of white horses pulled a silver carriage.	a pair of animals pulling together	a group on one side in an athletic contest
According to **tradition**, escaped prisoners founded the town.	belief or habit passed down over time	belief or story passed down over time that may or may not be true

Write About It!

You have read an article about rebuilding communities. Now you will write about the topic. Read the writing prompt. It gives your writing assignment.

WRITING RUBRIC

In your response, you should:

- Write a speech about rebuilding a community.

- Use information from the article to write your speech.

- Use at least one word from the Word Bank.

- Use correct grammar, usage, and mechanics.

Writing Prompt

Imagine your community has suffered a disaster. You have been asked to make a short, inspiring speech to your school on what it will take to come together and rebuild. Use ideas from the article and at least one word from the Word Bank.

community • culture • family • persuade • unify

Prewrite It

Once you are sure you understand the prompt, plan what you want to say.

1. Review your notes from the class discussion. Look for notes about what helps bring a community together to rebuild.

2. Reread the article. Make notes about the important points in the article on the organizer at the right.

3. Take another look at all your notes. Which are most important? Underline those notes to be sure to include them in your speech.

Why should we work together?

What answer will inspire people?

What can unite us?	How can we rebuild our community?

Give examples of rebuilding activities.

Draft It

Now use your plan to draft, or write, a speech to your school. The writing frame below will help you.

1. Write your speech by finishing the sentence prompts below.

2. Be sure that you use information and ideas from the article.

We should work together to rebuild because _____

_____

_____

_____.

To unite us, we need _____

_____

_____

_____.

To rebuild our community, we can _____

_____

_____

_____.

Check It and Fix It

After you have written your speech, check your work. Try to read it with a "fresh eye," as if you were reading it for the first time.

1. Is your speech written clearly and correctly? The checklist on the right will help you see.

2. Trade your work with a classmate. Talk about ways you both might improve your speeches. Use the ideas to revise your work.

3. For help with grammar, usage, and mechanics, go to the Handbook on pages 189–226.

Writing COACH

A speech's words and sentences should be easy to understand by people listening. Try writing your ideas and have a partner read them out loud. If you have problems understanding what the partner reads, revise the language.

✓ CHECKLIST

Evaluate your writing. A score of "5" is excellent. A score of "1" means you need to do more work. Then ask a partner to rate your work.

1. **Does the speech state thoughts clearly?**

   Me: 1 2 3 4 5
   Partner: 1 2 3 4 5

2. **Are there ideas from the article that support the points made?**

   Me: 1 2 3 4 5
   Partner: 1 2 3 4 5

3. **Is there at least one Word Bank word used?**

   Me: 1 2 3 4 5
   Partner: 1 2 3 4 5

4. **Are grammar, usage, and mechanics correct?**

   Me: 1 2 3 4 5
   Partner: 1 2 3 4 5

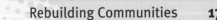

Vocabulary Workshop

Add these words to your personal word bank by practicing them.

 **community • culture • family • persuade • unify**

Your Choice

What other new words in the article would you like to remember? List them.

_____

_____

_____

Define It

Complete the chart below. Write each Word Bank word in the first column. In the second column, write your real-life meaning for the word. In the third column, write your connection to the word. Use the example as a guide.

Word	Real-Life Example	My Connection to the Word
community	The community of artists who live by me hold a street fair every summer.	Community reminds me of the get-togethers we have during the summer.

Show You Know

Respond to the items below to show you know how each boldface Word Bank word is used.

1. How could a **community** of people live in different neighborhoods? _____

   _____

2. How is the music of a country part of its **culture?** _____

   _____

3. Explain how your cousins are part of your **family**. _____

   _____

4. If you try to **persuade** someone, what are you trying to do? _____

   _____

5. If you **unify** a group of people, what are you doing? _____

   _____

Word Endings: *-ify*

- The word ending *-ify* can change a noun to a verb.

  Noun: unit

  Verb: unify

- In the sentences below, circle the correct word.

1. Urban gardens really (beauty, beautify) the city.

2. He is going to make a (speech, speechify) today.

3. Those clothes would (horror, horrify) your mother!

4. Festive lights (electric, electrify) our city during the

holidays.

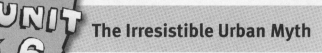

Write About It!

You have read an article about urban myths. Now you will write about the topic. Read the writing prompt. It gives your writing assignment.

In your response, you should:

- Write a welcome note for a Web site on urban myths.

- Support your opinion with ideas from the article.

- Use at least one word from the Word Bank.

- Use correct grammar, usage, and mechanics.

Writing Prompt

Write a welcome note for a new Web site on urban myths. You want people to know why the Web site exists and what purpose the myths serve. You also want them to know that the myths are not true. Use ideas from the article and at least one word from the Word Bank.

common • group • tradition • unique

Prewrite It

Once you are sure you understand the prompt, plan what you want to say.

1. Review your notes from the class discussion. Look for details about urban myths. Make notes on the organizer at the right.

2. Reread the article. Look for examples and facts that will be useful when you write. Include them in the organizer.

3. Take another look at all the notes you have listed. Circle the strongest ones. Make sure to include them in your welcome note.

Reasons People Enjoy Hearing and Telling Urban Myths	Purposes Urban Myths May Serve	Ways Urban Myths May Be Created

Draft It

Now use your plan to draft, or write, a welcome note to be featured on an urban myths Web site. The writing frame below will help you.

1. Begin by writing the name of the site or the words "Our Site."

2. Read each sentence prompt. Then finish each sentence with a point from your diagram. Be sure to use information from the article.

○ ○ ○

Welcome to _____

We think you will enjoy these urban myths because

_____

_____

We think myths serve a purpose. They _____

_____

But remember, these myths are _____

_____

_____

_____

_____

Check It and Fix It

After you have written your note, check your work. Try to read it with a "fresh eye." Imagine that you have never read the note before.

1. Is the welcome note written clearly and correctly? The checklist on the right will help you find out.

2. Trade your work with a classmate. Talk about ways you both might improve your welcome notes. Use the ideas to revise your work.

3. For help with grammar, usage, and mechanics, go to the Handbook on pages 189–226.

Ask your partner to imagine that he or she is at your new Web site for the first time. Then ask if the welcome note is helpful. A response from a reader can help you decide whether your writing is effective.

✔ **CHECKLIST**

Evaluate your writing. A score of "5" is excellent. A score of "1" means you need to do more work. Then ask a partner to rate your work.

1. **Is the Web site welcome note clear?**

   Me: 1 2 3 4 5
   Partner: 1 2 3 4 5

2. **Is information from the article used in the note?**

   Me: 1 2 3 4 5
   Partner: 1 2 3 4 5

3. **Is there at least one Word Bank word used?**

   Me: 1 2 3 4 5
   Partner: 1 2 3 4 5

4. **Are grammar, usage, and mechanics correct?**

   Me: 1 2 3 4 5
   Partner: 1 2 3 4 5

Vocabulary Workshop

Add these words to your personal word bank by practicing them.

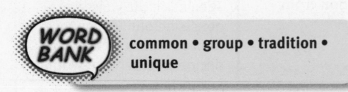

WORD BANK common • group • tradition • unique

Your Choice

What other new words in the article would you like to remember? List them.

_____

_____

_____

Define It

Complete the chart below using words from the Word Bank. First, tell what the word means. Then tell what the word does not mean. Use the example as a guide.

Word	What It Is	What It Is Not
common	when something happens a lot	when something happens once

Show You Know

Using all the Word Bank words, write a dialogue between two characters. Make sure the dialogue shows that you understand the words' meanings.

_____ : _____

_____

_____ : _____

_____

_____ : _____

_____

_____ : _____

_____

Partner Up

Exchange your dialogue with a partner. Choose roles and read the dialogues out loud. Do the dialogues sound like real conversations? If not, discuss how to make them sound more genuine and make the changes.

Word Origins

- Many English words come from other languages. The word *unit* comes from the Latin word *unus,* meaning "one." *Unit* means "one thing." The word *unique* also comes from *unus.*

- Circle the word in each sentence that you think comes from *unus.*

1. I joined the union so that the boss would treat me better.

2. A school song may seem unimportant, but I think it will unify the students.

3. The band usually sings in four-part harmony, but we sing this song in unison.

- Now, use one word that comes from the word *unus* in a sentence.

_____

_____

Write About It!

You have read an article about the importance of individual action. Now you will write about the topic. Read the writing prompt. It gives your writing assignment.

Writing Prompt

Imagine your school is hosting a photo exhibit called "Unsung Heroes." The exhibit is about people who have made a difference by helping others. Write a paragraph to be used as an exhibit introduction. Will you write about what one person can do alone or how one person can inspire others to work together? Use ideas from the article and at least one word from the Word Bank.

completely • diversity • environment • ethnicity • individual

WRITING RUBRIC

In your response, you should:

• Write an introduction to an exhibit about "unsung heroes."

• Use ideas from the article to help you organize your thoughts.

• Use at least one word from the Word Bank.

• Use correct grammar, usage, and mechanics.

Prewrite It

Once you are sure you understand the prompt, plan what you want to say.

1. Review your notes from the class discussion. If something is not clear in your memory, ask a classmate about it.

2. Reread the article. Make notes of details you think are important in the organizer at the right.

3. Take another look at your notes. Use them to help you decide what to write about.

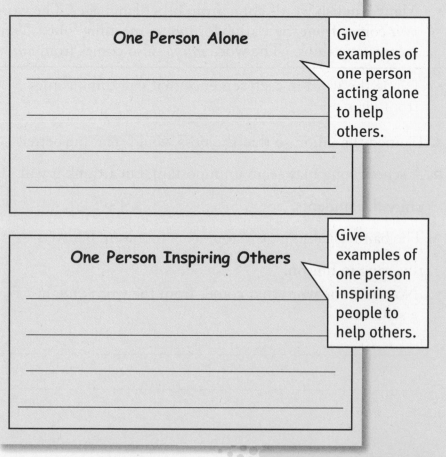

One Person Alone

> Give examples of one person acting alone to help others.

One Person Inspiring Others

> Give examples of one person inspiring people to help others.

Draft It

Now use your plan to draft, or write, an introduction to a photo exhibit. The writing frame below will help you.

1. State your opinion by underlining one of the options in the first sentence.

2. Use ideas and examples from the article to explain your thoughts.

Unsung Heroes

This exhibit shows that people can do the most good by

(acting alone, inspiring others to work together). This is

true because _____

_____

_____

_____

_____

_____

_____

_____

Check It and Fix It

After you have written the introduction, check your work. Imagine that you have never read the introduction before.

1. Is your introduction written clearly and correctly? The checklist on the right will help you figure that out.

2. Give your introduction to a classmate and read his or hers. Talk about ways you both might improve your writing. Use the ideas to revise your work.

3. For help with grammar, usage, and mechanics, go to the Handbook on pages 189–226.

When a subject is complicated, talking to a partner can help you understand better. Ask a partner questions about something you do not understand. See if your partner has any questions for you.

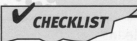

Evaluate your writing. A score of "5" is excellent. A score of "1" means you need to do more work. Then ask a partner to rate your work.

1. **Does the exhibit introduction state the opinion clearly?**

   Me: 1 2 3 4 5
   Partner: 1 2 3 4 5

2. **Is there information from the article that supports the opinion?**

   Me: 1 2 3 4 5
   Partner: 1 2 3 4 5

3. **Is there at least one Word Bank word used?**

   Me: 1 2 3 4 5
   Partner: 1 2 3 4 5

4. **Are grammar, usage, and mechanics correct?**

   Me: 1 2 3 4 5
   Partner: 1 2 3 4 5

Vocabulary Workshop

Add these words to your personal word bank by practicing them.

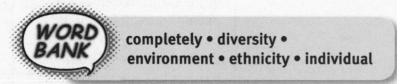

WORD BANK completely • diversity • environment • ethnicity • individual

Your Choice

What other new words in the article would you like to remember? List them.

_____

_____

_____

Define It

Complete the chart below. Write each Word Bank word, its meaning, and a word it reminds you of.

What It Means	completely
	Word It Reminds Me Of _____

What It Means	
	Word It Reminds Me Of _____

What It Means	
	Word It Reminds Me Of _____

What It Means	
	Word It Reminds Me Of _____

What It Means	
	Word It Reminds Me Of _____

Show You Know

For each word from the Word Bank, write a clue sentence for a partner to see if he or she can match it with the correct term. See the example for the word *completely*.

• This is how a person does something fully or to finish it off.

1. _____

_____

2. _____

_____

3. _____

_____

4. _____

_____

5. _____

_____

Word Origins

• When you see the word *individual*, do you think of any other word? The middle of the word, *divid*, looks a lot like the word *divide*, meaning "to separate into two or more parts." Both words come from the same Latin word, *dividere*, which means "to divide."

• In each sentence, circle the word that you think comes from *dividere*.

1. I'll give you a dime if you help me with this long-division problem.

2. At the end of the year, the company splits up its profits and pays out dividends at the stockholder's dinner.

3. We all tried to work together on the display, but Jorge kept saying divisive things.

Write About It!

You have read an article about trickster heroes. Now you will write about the topic. Read the writing prompt. It gives your writing assignment.

In your response, you should:

- Write a short chapter for a guide to cartoons.

- Use ideas from the article you read in your chapter.

- Use at least one word from the Word Bank.

- Use correct grammar, usage, and mechanics.

Writing Prompt

After reading "Trickster Appeal Revealed," what do you think about the appeal of tricksters? You are writing a short chapter for a guide to cartoons. Your chapter is called "Everyone Loves a Trickster." Explain why people like trickster characters. Use ideas from the article and at least one word from the Word Bank.

argue • culture • custom • family • unique

Prewrite It

Once you are sure you understand the prompt, plan what you want to say.

1. Review your notes from the class discussion. If there are details you do not remember clearly, talk to a classmate.

2. Reread the article. Make notes that will help you plan your chapter in the organizer on the right.

"Everyone Loves a Trickster"

Definition of a Trickster	Examples of Tricksters
_____	_____
_____	_____
_____	_____
_____	_____
_____	_____
_____	_____

When you define something, you tell what it is.

Reasons Why People Love Tricksters

1. _____

2. _____

3. _____

Give reasons you think people like tricksters.

Draft It

Now use your plan to draft, or write, a short article about tricksters. The writing frame below will help you.

1. Finish each thought with ideas from your notes.

2. Make sure you support your own thoughts with ideas from the article.

Talk with a partner about tricksters before you write your chapter. You may be able to come up with some examples of your own to add to those in the article.

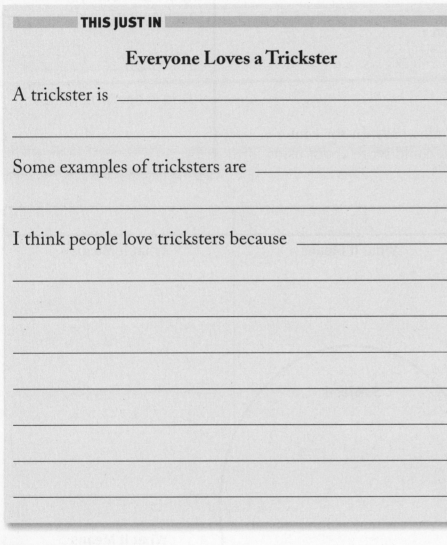

THIS JUST IN

Everyone Loves a Trickster

A trickster is _____

_____.

Some examples of tricksters are _____

_____.

I think people love tricksters because _____

_____

_____

_____

_____

_____

_____

_____

✔ CHECKLIST

Evaluate your writing. A score of "5" is excellent. A score of "1" means you need to do more work. Then ask a partner to rate your work.

1. **Does the chapter clearly describe tricksters and their appeal?**

   Me: 1 2 3 4 5
   Partner: 1 2 3 4 5

2. **Did ideas from the article help shape the chapter?**

   Me: 1 2 3 4 5
   Partner: 1 2 3 4 5

3. **Is there at least one Word Bank word used?**

   Me: 1 2 3 4 5
   Partner: 1 2 3 4 5

4. **Are grammar, usage, and mechanics correct?**

   Me: 1 2 3 4 5
   Partner: 1 2 3 4 5

Check It and Fix It

After you have written your chapter, check your work. Try to look at it with a "fresh eye."

1. Is the chapter clear and correct? The checklist on the right will help you find out.

2. Trade your work with a classmate. Talk about ways you both might improve your chapters. Revise your work if you think of something important.

3. For help with grammar, usage, and mechanics, go to the Handbook on pages 189–226.

Vocabulary Workshop

Add these words to your personal word bank by practicing them.

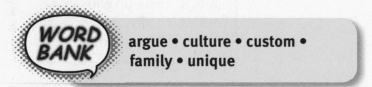

WORD BANK argue • culture • custom • family • unique

Your Choice

What other new words in the article would you like to remember? List them.

_____

_____

_____

Define It

Fill in the chart using the Word Bank words. In the center oval, write two or three subjects you could write about using the five Word Bank words.

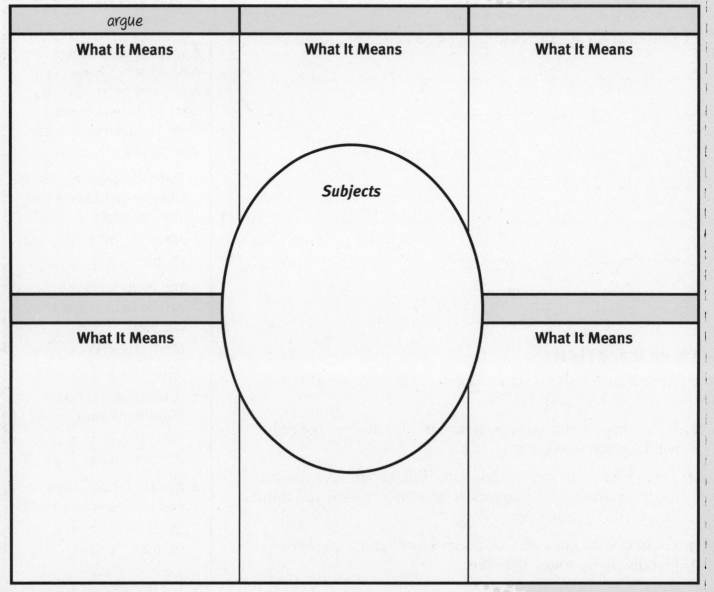

Show You Know

Write a comic strip in the space below using all the Word Bank words. Make sure the comic strip shows that you understand the words' meanings.

Partner Up

Trade comic strips with a partner. Read through each other's comic strips silently, and then read each aloud. Revise any language that is unclear.

Word Play

Using words with exact meanings can make your writing more lively and interesting. In the chart below, list some more specific words that mean about the same as the Word Bank words. Check a dictionary or thesaurus if you need to, and use the examples as models.

Word Bank Words	Similar Words
argue	plead, reason
custom	habit, tradition

Rewrite each of the sentences below, substituting one of your words for the boldface word.

1. Is it hard to **argue** with someone who wants to raise the driving age?

_____

2. My family has a **custom** of playing football after dinner.

_____

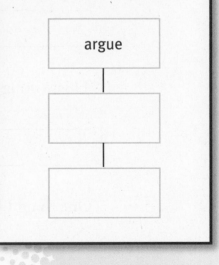

Add suffixes to the word *argue* to create two other words in the same word family.

argue

Writing Reflection

Community or individual—which is more important?

Look through your writing from this unit and choose the best piece. Reflect on this piece of writing by completing each sentence below.

My best piece of writing from this unit is _____

_____

I chose this piece because _____

_____

_____

While I was writing, one goal I had was _____

_____

I accomplished this goal by _____

_____

_____

This writing helped me think more about the Big Question because

_____

_____

One thing I learned while writing that can help me in the future is

_____

_____

GRAMMAR, USAGE, AND MECHANICS HANDBOOK

Nouns

A **noun** names a person, a place, or a thing.
Person: <u>Mona</u> is a <u>student</u>.
Place: My <u>school</u> is <u>Marson Middle School</u>.
Thing: That <u>article</u> is about <u>baseball</u>.

Regular Plurals

A **singular noun** names one person, place, or thing.
A **plural noun** names more than one person, place, or thing.
To form the plural of most nouns, add *-s* to the end of the noun.

Singular	Plural
one teenager	two teenager<u>s</u>
this computer	these computer<u>s</u>
that government	those government<u>s</u>
a site	many site<u>s</u>

 A noncount noun, which names something you cannot count, does not have a plural form. Some common noncount nouns are *clothing, equipment, furniture, information, knowledge,* and *water.*

Exercise: Regular Plurals

Highlight and fix the five mistakes in noun plurals.

(1) Animals help us in many ways. (2) Taking care of horses helps kid learn responsibility. (3) Dolphin provide therapy by swimming with people who have disabilities. (4) Dogs act as walking partner for blind people. (5) Some students find it easier to read aloud to therapy dogs than to classmate. (6) Pets help patients in hospitals and nursing home relax.

NOUNS continued

Special Noun Plurals

To make some nouns plural, you need to do more than add an *-s* ending. Use the chart to figure out how to spell these plurals.

Singular Noun Ending	Singular	Plural
When a noun ends in *ch*, *s*, *sh*, *x*, or *z*, add *-es*.	a lun**ch** one dres**s** that di**sh** this bo**x** each walt**z**	two lunch**es** many dress**es** those dish**es** these box**es** several waltz**es**
When a noun ends in a consonant + *y*, change the *y* to *i* and add *-es*.	a count**ry** one pen**ny** every ci**ty**	many count**ries** several pen**nies** ten ci**ties**
When a noun ends in *f* or *fe*, change the *f* to *v* and add *-s* or *-es*. Note: There are exceptions to this rule.	this lea**f** one kni**fe** a chie**f** one roo**f**	these lea**ves** two kni**ves** several chief**s** many roof**s**
When a noun ends in a consonant + *o*, add *-es*. Note: There are exceptions to this rule.	that her**o** a potat**o** one pian**o** an aut**o**	those her**oes** a dozen potat**oes** many pian**os** several aut**os**

WRITER'S ALERT! Do not use an apostrophe to form the plural of a noun.
Wrong: many belief's **Right:** many beliefs

Exercise: Special Noun Plurals

Highlight the misspelled noun plural in each sentence. Then fix the spelling mistake. Use the chart or a dictionary for help.

(1) Hurricanes and other natural disasters change the lifes of many people. **(2)** People who live in communitys hit by storms must come together to rebuild. **(3)** The Red Cross gives box's of food and clothes to people who are homeless. **(4)** Some volunteers fix damaged rooves. **(5)** Others donate autoes to friends and neighbors whose cars were ruined. **(6)** Everyday people become heros.

NOUNS continued

Irregular Plurals

Some plural nouns do not follow the rules. Memorize common **irregular plural nouns** like the ones below.

Singular	Plural
one <u>man</u>	two <u>men</u>
a <u>woman</u>	many <u>women</u>
that <u>child</u>	those <u>children</u>
this <u>person</u>	these <u>people</u>

Exercise: Irregular Plurals

Highlight and fix the misspelled plural in each sentence.

(1) The dentist's waiting room was filled with peoples. (2) Two womans chatted quietly. (3) A little boy had lost his front tooths.

(4) Two mens sat quietly waiting.

Possessive Nouns

A **possessive noun** shows ownership or relationship.
Ownership: John's coat = a coat that belongs to John
To make the possessive of a singular noun not ending in –s, add an apostrophe and an –s, as in **that boy's basketball.** To make a regular singular noun plural possessive, add –s and an apostrophe, as in **the boys' basketball team.**

The plural of irregular nouns does not end in s. Add an apostrophe and an –s to make the plural possessive.
Wrong: childrens' shoes   **Right:** children's shoes

Exercise: Possessive Nouns

Highlight and fix the possessive noun mistake in each sentence.

(1) We were excited about my oldest sisters birthday party.

(2) Then a blizzard hit, and our guests cars got stuck in the snow.

(3) Many of Marys friends could not come.

Pronouns

A **pronoun** takes the place of a noun or another pronoun. The word that a pronoun refers to is its **antecedent** (an tuh SEE duhnt).

<u>Jamal</u> plays the guitar. <u>He</u> is also learning the drums.
Antecedent   Pronoun

Subject and Object Pronouns

Pronouns take different forms depending on how they are used in sentences. A **subject pronoun** tells who or what a sentence is about. An **object pronoun** receives the action in a sentence or comes after a preposition (a word such as *for, from, in, on,* or *with*).

Subject Pronoun: <u>She</u> is a very fast swimmer.
Object Pronoun: The swim team gave <u>her</u> an award.
Object Pronoun: Swimming is fun for <u>her</u>.

	Singular Pronouns	**Plural Pronouns**
Used as Subjects	I you he, she, it	we you they
Used as Objects	me you him, her, it	us you them

Do not use pronouns ending in *self* as subject or object pronouns.
Wrong: She and <u>myself</u> are on the swim team.
Right: She and <u>I</u> are on the swim team.

Exercise: Subject and Object Pronouns
<u>Underline</u> the right pronoun form in each pair.

(1) Hurricane Katrina affected many people. (They, Them) needed help. **(2)** A famous actor helped by building houses for (they, them). **(3)** (He, him) founded a campaign called Make It Right. **(4)** More than 12,000 people have donated to the campaign, and (they, them) have given enough money to build more than fifty homes.

Pronouns continued

Pronouns in Compounds

Pronouns can be joined together with the word *and*. These are called **compound pronouns**.

Compound: <u>Sam and I</u> went to a movie.

Compound: The movie was exciting to <u>Sam and me.</u>

If you are not sure whether a pronoun in a compound should be in the subject form or the object form, leave out the noun. You may "hear" which form is right.

Example: My dad cooked hamburgers for ~~my brother and~~ (I, <u>me</u>).

Exercise: Pronouns in Compounds

Highlight and fix the pronoun mistake in each sentence.

(1) Ashlyn and me wanted to help our community. **(2)** Her and I decided to volunteer for a day at a local soup kitchen. **(3)** Serving people there was rewarding for her and I. **(4)** People said that she and me were a big help. **(5)** They want Ashlyn and I to volunteer again.

Possessive Pronouns

Possessive pronouns show who owns something. They can be used to describe nouns or in place of possessive nouns.

	Singular	**Plural**
Describer	<u>my</u> book <u>your</u> book <u>his</u>, <u>her</u>, <u>its</u> book	<u>our</u> books <u>your</u> books <u>their</u> books
Noun Substitute	<u>Mine</u> has my name in it. Did you forget <u>yours</u>? <u>His</u> and <u>hers</u> are missing.	<u>Ours</u> are here. <u>Yours</u> are there. <u>Theirs</u> are missing.

Exercise: Possessive Pronouns

Highlight and fix the pronoun mistake in each sentence.

(1) That book is mines. **(2)** It is not your's. **(3)** The other book is their. **(4)** Hers book is at home.

Pronouns continued

GRAMMAR HANDBOOK

Demonstrative Pronouns

The words *this*, *that*, *these*, and *those* are **demonstrative** (di MAHN struh tiv) **pronouns.** They point to a specific person, place, or thing. *This* and *these* point to who or what is near a speaker. *That* and *those* point to things farther away. *This* and *that* are singular. *These* and *those* are plural.

Never use *them* as a demonstrative pronoun.
Wrong: Bring me <u>them</u> books.
Right: Bring me <u>those</u> books.

Exercise: Demonstrative Pronouns

<u>Underline</u> the right pronoun to use in each pair.

(1) (This, That) bus stop is far away. **(2)** I would rather wait at (this, that) bus stop, here. **(3)** Have you ever ridden on one of (them, those) double-decker buses?

Indefinite Pronouns

Indefinite pronouns refer to people, places, or things that are not specifically identified. Some indefinite pronouns are always singular. Others are always plural.

Singular	anybody everybody no one	anyone everyone nothing	anything everything somebody	each neither someone	either nobody something
Plural	both	few	many	several	

Exercise: Indefinite Pronouns

Highlight the indefinite pronoun in each sentence. Write *S* above the pronoun if it is singular or *P* if it is plural.

(1) Everyone is nervous. **(2)** Most are there to play in the paintball playoffs. **(3)** Many have been in competitions before. **(4)** Anybody who practices regularly can play well. **(5)** Several have been playing paintball for years.

© Pearson Education, Inc. All rights reserved.

Pronouns   195

Pronouns continued

Pronoun-Antecedent Agreement

A pronoun and its antecedent—the word the pronoun stands for—must **agree,** or match. To match in number, both a pronoun and its antecedent must be singular or plural.

Wrong: <u>Nobody</u> raised <u>their</u> hand.
singular   plural

Right: <u>Nobody</u> raised <u>his or her</u> hand.
singular   singular

Use the chart to figure out how to make pronouns and their antecedents agree.

	Singular	Plural
First person	<u>I</u> have <u>my</u> pen.	<u>We</u> have <u>our</u> pens.
Second person	<u>You</u> have <u>your</u> pen.	<u>You</u> have <u>your</u> pens.
Third person	<u>He</u> has <u>his</u> pen.	<u>They</u> have <u>their</u> pens.

WRITER'S ALERT!

To avoid using the phrase *his or her,* make both the antecedent and the pronoun plural.
Singular: <u>Everybody</u> brought <u>his or her</u> ticket.
Plural: <u>All the students</u> brought <u>their</u> ticket<u>s</u>.

Exercise: Pronoun-Antecedent Agreement

Highlight and fix the pronoun mistake in each sentence.

(1) Everybody was supposed to bring their project to the science fair.

(2) Each student had their own space at the display table.

(3) Somebody forgot their project!

(4) No one wanted to go back to their classroom.

Pronouns continued

Relative Pronouns

A **relative pronoun** is used to introduce a clause (a group of words containing a verb and its subject). The relative pronoun *relates* the clause to the rest of the sentence.

Relative Clause: Marisa is the student <u>who won the award</u>.

relative
pronoun

Relative Pronouns
who, whom, whose, whoever, whomever, which, what, that

Use relative pronouns to combine two or three short, choppy sentences into one smooth sentence.

Choppy: The music is good. The music is on the radio.

Better: The music <u>that is on the radio</u> is good.

Exercise: Relative Pronouns

Use the relative pronoun in parentheses to combine each pair of sentences into one sentence.

1. (that) My poem was the shortest. It was in the contest.

_____.

2. (who) Judges read my poem. They liked it.

_____.

3. (who) I was one of only a few students. I wrote a nature poem.

_____.

4. (that) I am happy. I won.

_____.

Verbs

A **verb** expresses action or links important parts of a sentence together. Every sentence has at least one verb. The verb is the main word or group of words in the **predicate** (PRE duh kuht), which is the part of the sentence that tells about the subject.

Example: <u>Bob</u> <u>is</u> my brother.
The sentence is about Bob, so *Bob* is the subject. The verb *is* links *Bob* to *my brother,* which tells who Bob is. That makes *is* the verb in the predicate.

Example: <u>Bob</u> <u>writes</u> wonderful songs.
The sentence is about Bob, so *Bob* is the subject. The verb *writes* tells what Bob does, so *writes* is the verb in the predicate.

Action Verbs and Linking Verbs

Many **action verbs** name an action you can see—for example, *run, jump,* and *smile.* Other action verbs name an action you cannot see—for example, *think, wonder,* and *hope.* An action verb may stand alone with a subject to state a complete thought, or it may have an **object**—a person, place, or thing that receives or shows the result of the action.

Subject and Action Verb: <u>Darnella</u> <u>dances</u>.
                           subject   verb

Subject, Action Verb, and Object: <u>Carmelita</u> <u>plays</u> <u>piano</u>.
                          subject verb object

Linking verbs do not show action. Instead, they connect subjects with **complements**. Complements help complete the thought that subjects and their linking verbs begin to express. The most common linking verbs are forms of *to be: am, is, are, was, were, being, been.*

Thought Seems Incomplete: <u>Terrell</u> <u>is</u>.
Thought Is Complete: <u>Terrell</u> <u>is</u> a <u>firefighter</u>.

Exercise: Action Verbs and Linking Verbs

Highlight each action verb. <u>Underline</u> each linking verb.

(1) My cousin is a dancer. (2) She jumps high in the air. (3) She slides across the floor. (4) She and the other dancers are graceful.

(5) The crowd claps. (6) The dancers bow. (7) Everyone enjoyed the dance. (8) The evening was a success.

Verbs continued

Present Tense Verbs

The **tense** of a verb tells when something happened, happens, or will happen—in the past, the present, or the future. Use the **present tense** to express something that happens or exists in the present, happens regularly, or is always true.

Happens or Exists in the Present: I <u>see</u> that the sun <u>is setting</u>.

Happens Regularly: I <u>enjoy</u> the sunset nearly every day.

Is Always True: The sun <u>sets</u> in the west.

Use the chart below to form the present tense of **regular verbs** (verbs that follow regular rules). Notice that the form of a present tense verb depends on the subject that goes with it. If the subject is *he, she,* or *it,* the verb ends in *-s*. If the subject is *I, you, we,* or *they,* the verb does not end in *-s*.

Singular	Plural
I <u>like</u> you <u>like</u> he, she, it <u>likes</u>	we <u>like</u> you <u>like</u> they <u>like</u>

If a subject is a noun and you are not sure which verb form to use, change the noun into the pronoun that could substitute for it. Then use the chart.

Noun Subject: <u>Victor</u> (like, likes) rap.

Pronoun Subject: *Victor = he.* <u>Victor</u> (like, <u>likes</u>) rap.

Exercise: Present Tense Verbs

<u>Underline</u> the correct verb form in parentheses. Use the chart if you need to.

(1) Lin (take, takes) pictures of wildlife. **(2)** Rami (draw, draws) pictures of animals. **(3)** Lin and Rami (admire, admires) each other's work. **(4)** Rami (want, wants) to go to art school some day. **(5)** Their friends (say, says) they are talented artists. **(6)** In fact, the art teacher suggested that Lin and Rami (submit, submits) their art in a local art contest.

Verbs continued

Tricky Present Tense Verbs

Some verbs do not form the present tense in the regular way, by adding *-s*. The only way to learn tricky verbs like *have, do,* and *be* is to memorize them. Study the chart.

	Have	Do	Be
Singular	I <u>have</u> (<u>haven't</u>) you <u>have</u> (<u>haven't</u>) he, she, it <u>has</u> (<u>hasn't</u>)	I <u>do</u> (<u>don't</u>) you <u>do</u> (<u>don't</u>) he, she, it <u>does</u> (<u>doesn't</u>)	I am (<u>I'm</u> not) you are (<u>aren't</u>) he, she, it <u>is</u>, (<u>isn't</u>)
Plural	we <u>have</u> (<u>haven't</u>) you <u>have</u> (<u>haven't</u>) they <u>have</u> (<u>haven't</u>)	we <u>do</u> (<u>don't</u>) you <u>do</u> (<u>don't</u>) they <u>do</u> (<u>don't</u>)	we <u>are</u> (<u>aren't</u>) you <u>are</u> (<u>aren't</u>) they <u>are</u> (<u>aren't</u>)

These tricky verbs can stand alone as **main verbs,** or they can be helping verbs. A **helping verb** helps a main verb express action or give a statement.

Main Verb: Sinclair <u>has</u> a cell phone.

Helping Verb + Main Verb: Sinclair <u>has</u> <u>called</u> me on her phone.

Avoid using *ain't.*
Wrong: I <u>ain't</u> tired.
Right: I <u>am</u> <u>not</u> tired. OR <u>I'm</u> <u>not</u> tired.
Wrong: He <u>ain't</u> here.
Right: He <u>is</u> <u>not</u> here. OR He <u>isn't</u> here.

Exercise: Tricky Present Tense Verbs

Highlight and fix the six verb mistakes in the paragraph.

(1) I do not like to go to the movies with Niki. **(2)** She ain't afraid of scary films. **(3)** After I watch one, the creepy feeling don't go away. **(4)** I has been seeing the monster's face in my mind all day. **(5)** I am not walking home alone after school. **(6)** It sure do make me nervous. **(7)** I explained that watching scary movies ain't fun for me. **(8)** She have to go without me.

Verbs continued

Agreement with Compound Subjects

A **compound subject** is two or more subjects joined by the word *and* or *or*. When the subjects are joined by *and*, the compound subject is usually plural. To match, or agree with this compound subject, the verb must be in the plural form. When the subjects are joined by *or*, the verb must agree with the subject closer to it, whether singular or plural.

Compound with *And*: <u>Benoit and I</u> (is, <u>are</u>) friends.
Compound with *Or*: Benoit or <u>I</u> (<u>am</u>, is, are) happy to help.
Compound with *Or*: I or <u>Benoit</u> (am, <u>is</u>, are) happy to help.

Exercise: Agreement with Compound Subjects

Highlight and fix the three verb mistakes.

(1) Cameron and Shayne are shooting baskets. **(2)** Shayne and I is best friends. **(3)** Cameron or Shayne have been chosen team captain. **(4)** The coach or his assistant know which boy has been chosen. **(5)** You and I have to wait for the announcement.

Agreement in Questions

In most questions, all or part of the verb comes before the subject. The verb at the beginning of a question must agree with the subject.

Statement: <u>Thomasina</u> <u>is</u> <u>going</u> to the party.
          subject   verb

Question: <u>Is</u> <u>Thomasina</u> <u>going</u> to the party?
       verb   subject   verb

Exercise: Agreement in Questions

For each sentence, <u>underline</u> the right verb in parentheses.

(1) (Are, Is) you interested in working with the Urban Garden Program? **(2)** What (do, does) you want to help with? **(3)** What flowers (have, has) they planted? **(4)** Where (do, does) Marina want us to plant the tomatoes? **(5)** (Are, Is) there a shovel I can use?

Verbs continued

Past and Perfect Tenses

Use the **past tense** of a verb to show that something has already happened. To form the past tense of a regular verb, add an *-ed* ending.

Past: Yesterday, Lucie <u>called</u> me on her new phone.

Use the **present perfect tense** to show that something began in the past and is still happening or that happened at an indefinite time in the past. To form the present perfect, use the helping verb *has* or *have*.

Present Perfect: People <u>have</u> <u>used</u> cell phones since the 1970s.

Use the **past perfect tense** to express an action that was completed before another action in the past. To form the past perfect, use the helping verb *had*.

Past Perfect: I <u>had</u> already <u>left</u> the house when Lucie called.

	Present Perfect *have* or *has* + verb + *-ed*	Past Perfect *had* + verb + *-ed*
Singular	I <u>have</u> <u>walked</u> you <u>have</u> <u>walked</u> he, she, it <u>has</u> <u>walked</u>	I <u>had</u> <u>walked</u> you <u>had</u> <u>walked</u> he, she, it <u>had</u> <u>walked</u>
Plural	we <u>have</u> <u>walked</u> you <u>have</u> <u>walked</u> they <u>have</u> <u>walked</u>	we <u>had</u> <u>walked</u> you <u>had</u> <u>walked</u> they <u>had</u> <u>walked</u>

WRITER'S ALERT! The helping verb must agree with the subject.
Wrong: <u>Haven't</u> <u>he</u> listened to the news?
Right: <u>Hasn't</u> <u>he</u> listened to the news?

Exercise: Past and Perfect Tenses

Highlight and fix the verb mistake in each sentence.

(1) Anya has want to play piano all her life. **(2)** By the time she was ten, she had save enough money to buy a small keyboard. **(3)** Her parents realize how important it was to her, so they started to look for a piano. **(4)** A neighbor informs her parents that he did not have room to keep his piano. **(5)** They hasn't told Anya about the piano yet.

Verbs continued

Irregular Verbs 1: Past and Perfect of *To Be*

Irregular verbs do not take an -*ed* ending to form the past and perfect tenses. The most irregular verb in English is *to be*.

	Past Tense	Present Perfect Tense
Singular	I <u>was</u> (<u>wasn't</u>) you <u>were</u> (<u>weren't</u>) he, she, it <u>was</u> (<u>wasn't</u>)	I <u>have</u> (<u>haven't</u>) <u>been</u> you <u>have</u> (<u>haven't</u>) <u>been</u> he, she, it <u>has</u> (<u>hasn't</u>) <u>been</u>
Plural	we <u>were</u> (<u>weren't</u>) you <u>were</u> (<u>weren't</u>) they <u>were</u> (<u>weren't</u>)	we <u>have</u> (<u>haven't</u>) <u>been</u> you <u>have</u> (<u>haven't</u>) <u>been</u> they <u>have</u> (<u>haven't</u>) <u>been</u>

	Past Perfect Tense
Singular	I <u>had</u> (<u>hadn't</u>) <u>been</u> you <u>had</u> (<u>hadn't</u>) <u>been</u> he, she, it <u>had</u> (<u>hadn't</u>) <u>been</u>
Plural	we <u>had</u> (<u>hadn't</u>) <u>been</u> you <u>had</u> (<u>hadn't</u>) <u>been</u> they <u>had</u> (<u>hadn't</u>) <u>been</u>

Exercise: Irregular Verbs 1: Past and Perfect of *to Be*
Highlight and fix the four verb mistakes.

(1) The weather was terrible last week. (2) The forecast had been for good weather. (3) Then severe storms was spotted in the area.

(4) One thunderstorm was violent! (5) Soon, the roads was flooded.

(6) We was not able to go to school. (7) The governor have called for emergency help. (8) The sun has not shone here for days.

Irregular Verbs 2: Past and Perfect That Stay the Same

Some irregular verbs keep the same form for every tense. The most common are *cost, cut, hit, let, put, read, set,* and *shut.*
Present: I <u>read</u> everyday.
Past: Yesterday, I <u>read</u> the sports pages.
Present Perfect: I <u>have</u> <u>read</u> ten books this year.
Past Perfect: My mom gave me a book, but I <u>had</u> already <u>read</u> it.

Verbs continued

Irregular Verbs 3: Past and Perfect That Change Vowels

Some irregular verbs change only a vowel to go from present tense to past or perfect. Others add -*n* or -*en* to form the perfect tenses.

Present Tense	Past Tense	Perfect Tenses (has, have, had)
become	became	become
begin	began	begun
break	broke	broken
come	came	come
drink	drank	drunk
drive	drove	driven
forget	forgot	forgotten
give	gave	given
grow	grew	grown
know	knew	known
ride	rode	ridden
ring	rang	rung
rise	rose	risen
run	ran	run
see	saw	seen
sing	sang	sung
sit	sat	sat
speak	spoke	spoken
swim	swam	swum
write	wrote	written

Exercise: Irregular Verbs 3: Past and Perfect That Change Vowels

Highlight and fix the verb mistake in each sentence.

(1) The last time I speaked with Amber, she promised to visit during spring break. **(2)** She moved in January, and I have not saw her since. **(3)** Had she broke her promise? **(4)** Then the phone rung. **(5)** I knowed it was Amber. **(6)** She had not forgot after all.

Verbs continued

Irregular Verbs 4: Past and Perfect That Change Completely

Some verbs change their form completely to form the past or perfect tenses. Many of them (like *bring* and *buy*) have the same form for past and perfect tenses. A few (like *do* and *fly*) have different forms for past and perfect tenses.

Present Tense	Past Tense	Perfect Tenses (has, have, had)
bring	brought	brought
buy	bought	bought
catch	caught	caught
do	did	done
fight	fought	fought
find	found	found
fly	flew	flown
go	went	gone
sell	sold	sold
take	took	taken
teach	taught	taught
think	thought	thought

Exercise: Irregular Verbs 4: Past and Perfect That Change Completely

Highlight and fix the verb mistake in each sentence.

(1) My family just boughten a new house. (2) We had went to see a lot of houses before we found it. (3) At one house, jets flyed low overhead. (4) The real estate agent had brang us to a noisy neighborhood. (5) My parents thunk it was too noisy. (6) Then we find the perfect home for our family. (7) The house selled for a low price. (8) My parents done well.

Verbs continued

Verbs as Describers

Certain verb forms can act as describers. These **verbals** describe nouns or pronouns. Verbals can end in *-ing, -ed,* or, when the verb is irregular, the perfect form. Be sure to use the right ending or form.

Verbal with *-ing* ending: A freezing rain fell.

Verbal with *-ed* ending: Chantel wore faded jeans.

Verbal in Perfect Form: Her favorite jeans have a broken zipper.

Exercise: Verbs as Describers

Highlight and fix the three mistakes involving verbals.

(1) At my house, Saturday is cooking day. **(2)** My mom always makes fry chicken. **(3)** She also makes mash potatoes and chopped salad. **(4)** For dessert, we have froze yogurt or a freshly baked pie.

Future Tense

The **future tense** expresses action that will happen in the future. To form the future tense, use the helping verb *will* and a main verb.

Present: I walk to school every day.
Future: I will walk to soccer practice after school today.

Exercise: Future Tense

Change each underlined verb to future tense.

(1) We _____ go on a field trip to the Carnegie Museum.

(2) We _____ visit an art exhibition. **(3)** We _____ eat lunch in the museum cafeteria. **(4)** We _____ return to school at the end of the day.

Verbs continued

Progressive Tenses

The **progressive tense** expresses action in progress, or still happening. To form the present and past progressive, use a form of *to be* and a main verb with an *-ing* ending. To form the future progressive, add the helping word *will*.

Present Progressive: I <u>am</u> <u>biking</u>.
Past Progressive: I <u>was</u> <u>biking</u>.
Future Progressive: I <u>will be</u> <u>biking</u>.

Exercise: Progressive Tenses

Write a sentence to answer each question below. Make sure your answers are in the correct tenses.

1. What are you studying in English class?

_____

2. What were you doing early this morning?

_____

3. What will you be doing this weekend?

_____

Modals

Modals are helping verbs. They include *can, could, will, would, must, should, may, might,* and *ought to.* A main verb paired with a modal never takes an ending such as *-ed* or *-s*. It does not change form.

Wrong: I <u>should</u> **called** him.   **Right:** I <u>should</u> **call** him.
Wrong: She <u>can</u> **sings**.   **Right:** She <u>can</u> **sing**.

Exercise: Modals

Highlight and fix the verb mistake in each sentence.

(1) You should participated in school activities. (2) I would joining the drama club even if my friends were not in it. (3) Yvonne might plays soccer in the fall. (4) She would have play goalie if she had not been injured.

Adjectives

Adjectives describe nouns and pronouns. Adjectives answer these questions: *Which one? What kind? How many? How much?*

Which One: The <u>blue</u> coat is mine.

What Kind: It is a <u>wool</u> coat.

How Many: I own <u>two</u> coats.

How Much: That is <u>enough</u> coats for anyone.

Articles

The most often used adjectives are the **articles:** *a, an,* and *the. The* is called a **definite article,** because it is used to refer to a particular person, place, or thing. *A* and *an* are called **indefinite articles,** because they do not refer to a particular person, place, or thing.

Definite Article: Buy your ticket from <u>the</u> man in the booth.

Indefinite Article: <u>A</u> ticket costs $10.

Use *a* with words that begin with a consonant sound. Use *an* with words that begin with a vowel sound. (It is the *sound* that matters, not the spelling.)

A: <u>a</u> car, <u>a</u> song, <u>a</u> unit (*u* with the consonant *y* sound)

An: <u>an</u> ant, <u>an</u> olive, <u>an</u> umbrella (*u* with the vowel *u* sound)

Use *a* or *an* if the noun can be counted.
Example: I spilled <u>a</u> cup of coffee. (You can count a cup.)
Use *the* if the noun cannot be counted.
Example: I spilled <u>the</u> coffee. (You cannot count coffee that is not in a cup.)

Exercise: Articles

Highlight and fix the three mistakes involving articles.

(1) Every year, my school holds an art contest. **(2)** The judges are from an union of professional artists. **(3)** Any student can enter the drawing, photograph, or painting in the contest. **(4)** The judges decide which is the best artwork in each category. **(5)** I made an original work of art. **(6)** I mixed paint with a rain water from a puddle.

Adjectives continued

Adjectives That Compare

Adjectives can be used to make comparisons. Use the **comparative** (kuhm PER uh tiv) **adjective** form to compare two people, places, or things. To form the comparative of one-syllable adjectives and many two-syllable adjectives, add -*er*. To form the comparative of adjectives of three or more syllables, add the word *more* or *less* before the adjective.

One-Syllable Adjective: Sara is <u>younger</u> than I am.
Three-Syllable Adjective: I am <u>more</u> <u>athletic</u> than she is.

Use the **superlative** (soo PUHR luh tiv) **adjective** form to compare three or more people, places, or things. To form the superlative of one-syllable adjectives and many two-syllable adjectives, add -*est*. To form the superlative of adjectives of three or more syllables, add the word *most* or *least* in front of the adjective.

One-Syllable Adjective: Caryn is the <u>oldest</u> girl in our family.
Three-Syllable Adjective: She is our <u>most</u> <u>talented</u> musician.

 Some adjectives can take a comparative or superlative ending OR *more* or *most*. When in doubt, check a dictionary.

Exercise: Adjectives That Compare

Fill in each blank with the right form of the adjective in parentheses.

1. Otto is _____ than I am. **(old)**

2. His friend Al is the _____ player on the team. **(young)**

3. He is the _____ hitter in the league. **(famous)**

4. In our city, baseball is _____ than football. **(popular)**

5. The tickets for a baseball game are _____, too. **(cheap)**

Adjectives continued

Irregular Adjectives

Not all adjectives form comparisons in regular ways. The chart shows how to form common irregular adjectives.

Adjective	Comparative	Superlative
good, well	better	best
bad	worse	worst
many, much	more	most
little	less	least

Exercise: Irregular Adjectives

Fill in each blank with the right form of the adjective in parentheses.

1. Marcia is a _____ singer than I am. (**good**)

2. Marcia has won _____ contests than I have. (**many**)

3. She has won the _____ contests of all of us! (**many**)

4. Losing is the _____ thing about contests. (**bad**)

Double Comparisons

Never use *more* or *most* with an adjective that ends with *-er* or *-est*. This mistake in grammar is called a **double comparison.**
Wrong: My hometown is the <u>most</u> <u>bestest</u> place on earth.
Right: My hometown is the <u>best</u> place on earth.

Wrong: It is <u>more</u> <u>warmer</u> here than in Miami.
Right: It is <u>warmer</u> here than in Miami.

Exercise: Double Comparisons

Highlight and fix the three adjective mistakes.

(1) Summer is the best time of year. (2) It is light outside more longer than in the winter. (3) It is also more warmer. (4) We are the most happiest, because we have days off.

Adverbs

Adverbs describe verbs, adjectives, and other adverbs. Adverbs answer these questions: *How? When? Where? How often? How much?*

How: Jim spoke <u>quietly</u>.

When: He is <u>never</u> loud.

Where: He arrived <u>here</u> at five o'clock.

How often: He <u>usually</u> arrives at four o'clock.

The *-ly* Adverb Ending

Many adverbs are formed by adding *-ly* to the end of an adjective.

Example: quiet + ly = quietly

Not all adverbs end in *-ly*, however, and not every word that ends in *-ly* is an adverb. For example, the word *friendly* ends in *-ly*, but it is an adjective, not an adverb.

The word *real* is an adjective. The word *really* is an adverb. Use *really* when you are describing an adjective.

Wrong: Sherelle is <u>real</u> happy.

Right: Sherelle is <u>really</u> happy.

Exercise: The *-ly* Adverb Ending

Add *-ly* to each adjective in parentheses to form an adverb.

1. My dog barks _____. **(loud)**

2. She tugs _____ on the leash. **(constant)**

3. She wags her tail _____. **(happy)**

4. She runs home _____. **(quick)**

5. She _____ eats her dinner. **(enthusiastic)**

Adverbs continued

Good and *Well*

Use the adjective *good* to describe people, places, and things.

Example: That is a good song.

Well is usually an adverb that is used to describe action verbs and adjectives. Also use *well* as an adjective to describe someone's health.

Example: The band played well.

Example: *Jen* felt well after a good night's rest.

Exercise: *Good* and *Well*

Highlight and fix the two mistakes in the use of *good* and *well*.

(1) I did not feel good, so I stayed home. **(2)** I wanted to do good on the test, so I studied. **(3)** I got a good grade!

Double Negatives

Do not form a **double negative** by using two negative words in the same clause. The adverb *not* is negative. So are contractions that contain the word *not* (*can't, don't, haven't, isn't, wasn't,* and so on). To fix a double negative, change one of the negatives to a positive, or drop one of the negative words.

Wrong: I don't have no money.

Right: I do not have any money. OR I have no money.

Negatives	Positives
never	ever
nobody, no one	somebody, someone
none	some
nothing	something, anything
nowhere	somewhere
hardly, barely	_____

Exercise: Double Negatives

Highlight and fix the double negative in each sentence.

(1) I didn't get hardly any sleep. **(2)** I wasn't never that tired before.

(3) I didn't want to do nothing.

Prepositions

A **preposition** (pre puh ZI shuhn) shows the relationship between a noun or pronoun and another word in a sentence.

Example: The stars shone <u>above</u> us.
Example: We sat <u>on</u> a bench <u>beside</u> the lake.

Prepositions					
about	among	beneath	for	on	under
above	around	beside	from	onto	underneath
across	at	between	in	over	until
after	before	beyond	into	through	with
against	behind	by	near	to	within
along	below	during	of	toward	without

Prepositional Phrases

A **prepositional phrase** is a group of words that go together and that begin with a preposition and end with a noun or pronoun. The noun or pronoun at the end of the phrase is called the **object of the preposition.**

Prepositional Phrase: The moon rose <u>over the calm lake</u>.
                                          preposition   object

Exercise: Prepositional Phrases

<u>Underline</u> the prepositional phrase in each sentence below.

(1) There is a new computer lab in my school. **(2)** The lab has

different kinds of equipment. **(3)** After school, I answer my e-mail.

(4) The messages from my friends are often funny. **(5)** I write funny

replies to those messages.

Conjunctions

Conjunctions (kuhn JUHNG shuhns) connect, or join, words or groups of words. There are three kinds of conjunctions:

1. coordinating

2. correlative

3. subordinating

Coordinating Conjunctions

Coordinating (koh AWR duh nay ting) **conjunctions** connect similar words or groups of words. They can link parts of sentences or whole sentences. The coordinating conjunctions are as follows:

Coordinating Conjunctions
and, but, for, nor, or, so, yet

Sentence Parts: Kim and her mom went on a trip.

Sentences: They went to Ohio, and they saw the Columbus Zoo.

Exercise: Coordinating Conjunctions

Highlight the coordinating conjunction in each sentence.

1. On Saturday, my family and I went bowling.

2. We hoped to bowl a few games, but the bowling alley was crowded.

3. My mom kept score for us, so she did not play.

4. I wanted to get a higher score than my dad or my brother.

5. My dad helped me improve my approach, yet I still did not beat him.

6. He is a skillful bowler, and he is very competitive.

7. I beat my brother but not my dad.

8. I like to go bowling with my family, for we always have a lot fun.

Conjunctions continued

Subordinating Conjunctions

A **subordinating** (suh BAWR duh nay ting) **conjunction** introduces and connects a subordinate clause to a main clause.

Subordinating Conjunctions			
after	because	since	until
although	before	so that	when
as	even though	than	where
as if	if	though	whereas
as though	in order that	unless	while

Example: While we were in Chicago, we visited museums.

                 subordinate clause   main clause

Exercise: Subordinating Conjunctions

Highlight the subordinating conjunction in each sentence and underline the subordinate clause.

(1) When I grow up, I want to be a nurse. **(2)** I would like to work in a hospital, because I like helping people. **(3)** Though nursing is hard work, it is very rewarding.

Correlative Conjunctions

Correlative (kuh RE luh tiv) **conjunctions** work in pairs.

both . . . and	either . . . or
not only . . . but also	neither . . . nor

Example: Both Lia and Raj are in the chess club.
Example: Neither Lia nor Raj likes to lose.

Exercise: Correlative Conjunctions

Highlight the pair of correlative conjunctions in each sentence.

(1) Both my mom and my dad are carpenters. **(2)** My mom not only builds but also paints. **(3)** Neither my mom nor my dad cooks!

Sentences

A **complete sentence** is a group of words that has a subject and a predicate and that expresses a complete thought. The **subject** tells who or what the sentence is about. The predicate tells what the subject is or does.

Complete Sentence: <u>Josephina</u> <u>overslept this morning</u>.

            subject   predicate

There are four types of sentences.

1. A **declarative** (di KLER uh tiv) sentence makes a statement.

- <u>Josephina</u> <u>missed</u> her bus.

2. An **imperative** (im PER uh tiv) sentence gives an order.

- <u>Set</u> the alarm. (The "understood" subject is <u>you</u>.)

3. An **exclamatory** (iks KLA muh tawr ee) sentence shows emotion.

- What a nightmare <u>she</u> <u>had</u>!

4. An **interrogative** (in tuh RAH guh tiv) sentence asks a question.

- What time <u>did</u> <u>she</u> <u>go</u> to bed last night?

Clauses

A **clause** is a group of words that contains a verb and its subject. A **main clause** can stand alone as a sentence. A **subordinate clause** begins with a subordinating conjunction. A subordinate clause cannot stand alone. It must be joined to a main clause.

Main Clause: <u>Lenny</u> <u>is</u> afraid to speak in public.
Subordinate Clause: because <u>he</u> <u>is</u> very shy
Sentence: Lenny is afraid to speak in public because he is very shy.

Exercise: Clauses

<u>Underline</u> the subordinate clause in each sentence below.

(1) Lara gave her oral report when I gave mine. **(2)** She reported on the race horse Seabiscuit, because she loves horses. **(3)** As she talked, I tried to concentrate. **(4)** It was my turn after Lara spoke. **(5)** Though I tried to be calm, I felt nervous. **(6)** Lara is a more experienced public speaker than I am. **(7)** Before I knew it, I had to give my report. **(8)** My report went much better than I expected!

Sentences continued

Run-on Sentences

A **run-on sentence** is a common kind of mistake in writing. A run-on happens when two or more sentences are written as one sentence. There are three kinds of run-on sentences:

1. Main clauses are separated only by a comma.

- Roy walked home, it was autumn.

2. Main clauses are not separated by any punctuation.

- The sky was blue the leaves were red and gold.

3. Main clauses are separated by a coordinating conjunction, but the comma before the conjunction is missing.

- He felt like running but he did not want to make any noise.

Here are two ways to fix a run-on sentence.

Fix 1: Separate the main clauses, or sentences, with a period.

- Roy walked home. It was autumn.

Fix 2: Add a comma and a coordinating conjunction (if the sentences are not already separated by a coordinating conjunction).

- The sky was blue, and the leaves were red and gold.

- He felt like running, but he did not want to make any noise.

Exercise: Run-on Sentences

Fix the three run-on sentences below. There is more than one right way to fix each sentence.

(1) Pizza is a very old kind of food it has probably been around since the Stone Age. (2) Soldiers used to cook pizza on their shields, but it was topped with dates instead of sausage. (3) Tomatoes were not brought to Europe until the 1500s so the first Italian pizzas did not have tomato sauce. (4) Today, pizza is one of the most popular foods in the world millions of people eat it.

Sentences continued

Fragments

A **sentence fragment** is an incomplete sentence that is capitalized and punctuated as if it were complete. Common reasons for fragments are as follows:

1. The sentence is missing a subject.

Fragment: <u>Went</u> to a storytelling festival.
Complete: <u>Al and Beatrice</u> <u>went</u> to a storytelling festival.

2. The sentence is missing a predicate.

Fragment: <u>Al and Beatrice</u> to a storytelling festival.
Complete: <u>Al and Beatrice</u> <u>went</u> to a storytelling festival.

3. A subordinate clause is not connected to a main clause.

Fragment: When they got to the festival.
Complete: When they got to the festival, they saw some friends.

Fragment: Until the very end.
Complete: They did not leave until the very end.

Exercise: Fragments

Follow the directions in parentheses to fix each fragment.

1. (Add a subject.) _____ love to eat at new restaurants.

2. (Add a predicate.) I _____ to a new restaurant at least twice a month.

3. (Add a main clause.) _____ since they serve my favorite kind of food.

4. (Add a predicate.) What kind of food _____ your favorite?

5. (Add a main clause.) Whatever kind of food you prefer,

_____

Capitalization

Capitalize proper nouns and proper adjectives. A **proper noun** names a specific person, place, or thing. A **common noun** is a general name for a person, place, or thing. A **proper adjective** is an adjective formed from a proper noun.

Common	Proper
man	Damion
school	Wilson Middle School

Capitalize the following.

1. The proper name or title of a person:

- <u>S</u>ue, <u>D</u>ad, <u>M</u>s. <u>S</u>mith, <u>D</u>etective <u>J</u>ones, <u>P</u>resident <u>A</u>dams

2. The proper name of a place:

- <u>C</u>hicago, <u>U</u>tah, <u>F</u>rance, <u>M</u>ain <u>S</u>treet, the <u>S</u>ears <u>T</u>ower

3. A proper adjective:

- <u>A</u>merican, <u>M</u>exican, <u>C</u>hinese

4. The first word of a sentence:

- <u>T</u>he night was dark.

5. The salutation of a letter and the first word of the closing:

- <u>D</u>ear <u>S</u>ir: • <u>S</u>incerely yours,

6. The first word, last word, and all main words in the title of a work:

- *<u>T</u>he <u>S</u>ound of <u>M</u>usic*

Exercise: Capitalization

Highlight and fix the capitalization mistake or mistakes in each item.

(1) Dear aunt cicily,

(2) We had the best time in New york! **(3)** We went to see the statue of liberty. **(4)** then we went to see a play. **(5)** It was called a Raisin in the sun. **(6)** Afterward, we ate italian food.

Punctuation

Punctuation helps readers understand how sentences should be read. **Punctuation marks** include commas, apostrophes, quotation marks, and end marks (periods, question marks, and exclamation points).

A **comma** signals a pause or separates parts of a sentence:
• When the phone rang, he answered.
• Berkeley, California, is her home.

An **apostrophe** can show possession, show where letters are missing in a contraction, or show that a letter or number is plural.
• Sara's ears almost froze when she didn't wear her hat.
• Several members of the class got straight A's.

Quotation marks set off someone's exact words. They are also used to set off titles of articles, short stories, and episodes of TV shows.
• "What did you say?" Homer asked.
• My favorite show is "My Best Friends."

End Marks

An **end mark** goes at the end of a sentence.
A **period** ends a complete sentence that makes a statement.
• Roz went to school early today.

A **question mark** ends a direct question.
• Why did she go early?

An **exclamation point** ends a sentence that shows strong emotion.
• Do not spill that juice!

 Put periods and commas inside closing punctuation marks. "I am glad," Maria said, " to meet you at last."

Exercise: End Marks

Add the correct end mark to each sentence.

(1) Have you ever baked a pie (2) We baked one today in cooking

class (3) I almost burned my pie (4) The juice spilled in the oven

(5) Smoke was everywhere

Punctuation continued

Commas

Use commas in the following situations:

1. To separate three or more items in a series:

- They walked past shops, houses, and parks.

2. To set off names and titles used in direct address:

- "Have you seen my CD, Tim? No, Terrell, I haven't."

3. To set off dates and addresses:

- On July 25, 1999, my sister was born in St. George, Utah.

4. After an introductory word, phrase, or clause:

- Finally, the day ended. At last, we relaxed. If you want, sleep.

5. To set off groups of words that explain or rename:

- Soccer, my favorite sport, involves a lot of running.

6. To separate main clauses joined by a coordinating conjunction:

- Ron did his homework, but Ken did not do his.

WRITER'S ALERT!

Do not use a comma to separate the parts of a compound predicate, except to prevent misreading.
Wrong: Ron sings well, and plays the guitar even better.
Right: Ron sings well and plays the guitar even better.

Exercise: Commas

Add the missing comma or commas to each sentence.

(1) Have you ever been to a krumping contest Frank? **(2)** Really the contests are a lot of fun. **(3)** Groups of dancers perform dance routines and judges rate how well the groups did. **(4)** I went to my first krumping contest on June 10 2008 in my hometown. **(5)** Russ my best friend went with me. **(6)** Russ Allan and I enjoy krumping. **(7)** We have traveled as far as Detroit Michigan to see the contests. **(8)** When the audience cheers it feels great. **(9)** In fact it is one of the greatest feelings ever!

Punctuation continued

Apostrophes

Use an apostrophe to show letters are missing in a contraction.
- aren't (are not), can't (cannot), haven't (have not).

Do not confuse contractions with possessives that sound like them. A possessive pronoun never takes an apostrophe.
- The cat licked its fur, and now it's clean.

Also use an apostrophe to show possession.
- Cal's dad drove him to school. Some kids' homes are far from school.

Exercise: Apostrophes

Fix the apostrophe mistake in each sentence.

(1) Steves favorite video game is Soap Box Derby. **(2)** Its a cross between racing cars and building race cars. **(3)** Hes playing the game right now. **(4)** May I borrow your's?

Quotation Marks

Use quotation marks before and after someone's exact words.
Do not use them to set off an indirect quotation.

Direct Quotation: "I'm ready," Shari said, "to work."
Indirect Quotation: Shari said she was ready to work.

Set off titles of articles, short stories, and episodes of TV shows with quotation marks.

Title of Essay: Did you read the article "Sports Shorts"?
Title of Story: My favorite story is "Amigo Brothers."

Exercise: Quotation Marks

Add quotation marks where needed in the sentences below.

1. Did you do your homework? Mickey asked.

2. We are supposed to read the story Two Kinds.

3. I started to read it, Bob said, but I fell asleep.

Spelling

Though some words are spelled exactly the way they sound, many are not. Use these rules to help guide your spelling. When in doubt, turn to a dictionary for help.

1. Put *i* before *e* except after *c* or the sound *ay.*

Examples: bel<u>ie</u>ve, fr<u>ie</u>nd, p<u>ie</u>ce, rel<u>ie</u>f, sh<u>ie</u>ld
Examples: c<u>ei</u>ling, rec<u>ei</u>pt, rec<u>ei</u>ve, n<u>ei</u>ghbor, w<u>ei</u>ght

2. When adding an ending that starts with a vowel (like *-ed, -er,* or *-ing*), double these final consonants: *b, d, g, l, m, n, p, r,* and *t.*

Examples: sob<u>bed</u>, nag<u>ged</u>, begin<u>ner</u>, win<u>ner</u>, tap<u>ping</u>, bat<u>ting</u>

3. When adding *-ed, -es, -ing,* or *-y* to a word that ends with a silent *e,* drop the *e.*

Examples: bake + -ed = bak<u>ed</u>, tape + -ing = tap<u>ing</u>, rose + y = ros<u>y</u>

4. When a word ends in a consonant plus *y,* change the *y* to *i* before adding an ending like *-ed, -es, -est,* or *-ly.*

Examples: supply + -ed = suppl<u>ied</u>, fly + -es = fl<u>ies</u>,
easy + -est = eas<u>iest</u>, happy + *ly* = happ<u>ily</u>

5. When a word ends in a vowel plus *y,* do not change the *y* to *i* when adding *-ed, -er,* or *-s.*

Examples: delay<u>ed</u>, play<u>er</u>, s<u>ays</u>, k<u>eys</u>, t<u>oys</u>, g<u>uys</u>

Exercise: Spelling
Highlight and fix the spelling mistake in each sentence.

(1) Coach, did you recieve the shipment of shoes for the soccer team? **(2)** Did you order other supplys we need? **(3)** My nieghbor Lonny wants to play this year. **(4)** Last year, he played sloppyly. **(5)** This year, he amazeed me with his speed. **(6)** Also, Sal's footwork is dazzleing. **(7)** All the plaiers are ready for the season. **(8)** Some of the guyes have been training for months. **(9)** This will be the crazyest season ever for our team. **(10)** I predict that we'll be winers by December.

Commonly Confused Words

The words on this list give many writers trouble. Use the list for help in figuring out the right word to use.

accept, except
Accept means "to agree to" or "to welcome." *Except* means "but."

- I hope everyone will <u>accept</u> the new student to our class.
- We go to school every day <u>except</u> Saturday and Sunday.

affect, effect
Affect means "to influence" or "to have an impact on." *Effect* means "result."

- I hope the cancelled flight will not <u>affect</u> your travel plans.
- A high fever was one <u>effect</u> of the disease.

a lot
The expression *a lot* means "a large number" or "a large amount." It must be written as two words.

- <u>A lot</u> of people came to the championship game.

all ready, already
The expression *all ready* means "completely prepared." It is written as two words. *Already* means "before now." It is one word.

- Dinner was <u>all ready</u> by the time the guests arrived.
- I got to the stadium so late the game was <u>already</u> over.

amount, number
The word *amount* describes a quantity that cannot be counted. Use *number* to describe things that can be counted.

- The cake contained a large <u>amount</u> of sugar.
- She was impressed by the <u>number</u> of tickets that were sold.

beside, besides
Beside refers to someone or something next to another. *Besides* means "as well as" or "other than."

- She stood <u>beside</u> the lamppost, waiting for the bus.
- <u>Besides</u> math, I also like to study science and English.

Commonly Confused Words continued

can, may
The verb *can* means "is able." *May* means "is allowed."

- She <u>can</u> repair the car because she has the right tools.
- He <u>may</u> watch the concert because he has a ticket.

fewer, less
Fewer compares numbers of people or things that can be counted. *Less* compares amounts or quantities that cannot be counted.

- The class had <u>fewer</u> boys than girls.
- My new car uses <u>less</u> gas than my old one.

like, as
Like is a preposition, and it should be followed by an object. *As* is a conjunction, and it should be followed by a clause, which contains both a subject and a verb.

- She sings <u>like</u> a bird.
- She sings <u>as</u> a <u>bird</u> <u>would sing</u>.

loose, lose
Loose is an adjective (meaning "weakly connected" or "unattached"). *Lose* is always a verb (meaning the opposite of "to win" or "to find").

- The <u>loose</u> stones in the wall fell to the street.
- The team that does not practice is sure to <u>lose</u> the game.

rise, raise
Rise means "to go up." *Raise* is used with an object, and it means "to lift or force up."

- Please <u>raise</u> your hand if you have a question.
- The sun will <u>rise</u> at seven o'clock tomorrow morning.

sit, set
Sit means "to be seated." *Set* means "to put or place."

- I will <u>sit</u> at the table during dinner.
- I will <u>set</u> the dishes on the table.

Commonly Confused Words continued

than, then
Than is a conjunction used to compare one person or thing with another. *Then* is an adverb that means "after that" or "next."

- An elephant is larger <u>than</u> a mouse.
- First beat the eggs, and <u>then</u> add the milk.

their, there, they're
Their is a possessive pronoun, which expresses ownership or relationship. *There* expresses where something or someone is. *They're* is the contraction for *they are*.

- <u>They're</u> going to swim during <u>their</u> visit to Florida.
- The weather is sunny and warm <u>there</u>.

to, too, two
To expresses direction or location. *Too* means "as well" or "in addition." *Two* is the number between one and three.

- I bought <u>two</u> tickets for the concert, so you can come, <u>too</u>.
- We should take a bus <u>to</u> the theater.

who, whom
Who is the subject of the verb that follows it. *Whom* is an object, either receiving the action of a verb or ending a prepositional phrase.

- <u>Who</u> wrote the letter?
- I did not know <u>whom</u> to call.
- For <u>whom</u> did you ask?

who's, whose
Who's is the contraction for *who is*. *Whose* is a possessive pronoun, expressing ownership or relationship.

- <u>Who's</u> going to be our teacher next year?
- Do you know <u>whose</u> bicycle this is?

Editing Checklist

Use this checklist as you edit your writing. (You can also use this checklist to edit a partner's work.) Keep track as you complete each step.

1. I found misspelled words and used strategies to spell them correctly.

2. I checked to be sure that I used the correct homophone, such as *your/you're, to/too/two,* and *they're/their/there.*

3. I reread each sentence to make sure that I did not leave out words.

4. I fixed run-on sentences and sentence fragments.

5. I looked to be sure that each new idea started a new paragraph.

6. I correctly placed periods, question marks, exclamation marks, and commas where they belong.

7. I began each sentence with an uppercase letter.

8. I used uppercase letters for names of people and places and for proper nouns.

9. I made sure that subjects and verbs in sentences agree.

My editing goals:

_____

_____

_____

_____

_____

_____

Proofreaders' Marks

Use these marks as you review your own or a partner's writing.

℘	Delete	∧	Insert here
◡	Close up; delete space	⋏	Insert comma
(stet)	Let it stand	∨	Insert apostrophe
#	Insert space	⋎⋎	Insert quotation marks
¶	Begin new paragraph	⊙	Insert period
(sp)	Spell out	(set)?	Insert question mark
(lc)	Set in lowercase	⟨∘⟩	Insert colon
(caps)	Set in capital letters	=	Insert hyphen

Dear Jurors,

I think you should put you're trust in forensic science.
One reason for is that a witness to a crime may not
remember all the details. Proove from science is reliable. Its
hard to argue with a fingerprint or dna. Another reason
is that science keeps getting gooder. Compared to a
long time ago scientists can find out more information.
About crime scenes. If you were accused of a crime,
wouldn't you want science on your side.

Personal Word Bank

Use the Word Bank to keep track
of the "Your Choice" words from the articles.

For each word you add, do the following:

- Write the word in the box.

- Rate how well you understand it.

  1 = I do not know this word.

  2 = I have seen or heard this word.

  3 = I could use this word in a sentence.

  4 = I could teach this word to someone else.

- Write the definition in your own words.

- Write an example of the word or a connection you have with it.

- Use the word! Write with it, speak with it, and pay attention if
  you find it in your reading. Then go back to your rating and see if
  you can improve it.

Word: _____ **My Understanding** 1 2 3 4 **Definition:** _____ **Example or Connection:** _____ _____ _____	**Word:** _____ **My Understanding** 1 2 3 4 **Definition:** _____ **Example or Connection:** _____ _____ _____
Word: _____ **My Understanding** 1 2 3 4 **Definition:** _____ **Example or Connection:** _____ _____ _____	**Word:** _____ **My Understanding** 1 2 3 4 **Definition:** _____ **Example or Connection:** _____ _____ _____
Word: _____ **My Understanding** 1 2 3 4 **Definition:** _____ **Example or Connection:** _____ _____ _____	**Word:** _____ **My Understanding** 1 2 3 4 **Definition:** _____ **Example or Connection:** _____ _____ _____

Personal Word Bank

Word: _____ My Understanding
                        1 2 3 4

Definition: _____

Example or Connection: _____
_____
_____

Word: _____ My Understanding
                        1 2 3 4

Definition: _____

Example or Connection: _____
_____
_____

Word: _____ My Understanding
                        1 2 3 4

Definition: _____

Example or Connection: _____
_____
_____

Word: _____ My Understanding
                        1 2 3 4

Definition: _____

Example or Connection: _____
_____
_____

Word: _____ My Understanding
                        1 2 3 4

Definition: _____

Example or Connection: _____
_____
_____

Word: _____ My Understanding
                        1 2 3 4

Definition: _____

Example or Connection: _____
_____
_____

Word: _____ My Understanding
                        1 2 3 4

Definition: _____

Example or Connection: _____
_____
_____

Word: _____ My Understanding
                        1 2 3 4

Definition: _____

Example or Connection: _____
_____
_____

Word: _____ My Understanding
                        1 2 3 4

Definition: _____

Example or Connection: _____
_____
_____

Word: _____ My Understanding
                        1 2 3 4

Definition: _____

Example or Connection: _____
_____
_____

Personal Word Bank

Word: _____
My Understanding
1 2 3 4

Definition: _____

Example or Connection: _____
_____
_____

Word: _____
My Understanding
1 2 3 4

Definition: _____

Example or Connection: _____
_____
_____

Word: _____
My Understanding
1 2 3 4

Definition: _____

Example or Connection: _____
_____
_____

Word: _____
My Understanding
1 2 3 4

Definition: _____

Example or Connection: _____
_____
_____

Word: _____
My Understanding
1 2 3 4

Definition: _____

Example or Connection: _____
_____
_____

Word: _____
My Understanding
1 2 3 4

Definition: _____

Example or Connection: _____
_____
_____

Word: _____
My Understanding
1 2 3 4

Definition: _____

Example or Connection: _____
_____
_____

Word: _____
My Understanding
1 2 3 4

Definition: _____

Example or Connection: _____
_____
_____

Word: _____
My Understanding
1 2 3 4

Definition: _____

Example or Connection: _____
_____
_____

Word: _____
My Understanding
1 2 3 4

Definition: _____

Example or Connection: _____
_____
_____

Word: _____ | My Understanding 1 2 3 4

Definition: _____

Example or Connection: _____

_____

_____

Word: _____ | My Understanding 1 2 3 4

Definition: _____

Example or Connection: _____

_____

_____

Word: _____ | My Understanding 1 2 3 4

Definition: _____

Example or Connection: _____

_____

_____

Word: _____ | My Understanding 1 2 3 4

Definition: _____

Example or Connection: _____

_____

_____

Word: _____ | My Understanding 1 2 3 4

Definition: _____

Example or Connection: _____

_____

_____

Word: _____ | My Understanding 1 2 3 4

Definition: _____

Example or Connection: _____

_____

_____

Word: _____ | My Understanding 1 2 3 4

Definition: _____

Example or Connection: _____

_____

_____

Word: _____ | My Understanding 1 2 3 4

Definition: _____

Example or Connection: _____

_____

_____

Word: _____ | My Understanding 1 2 3 4

Definition: _____

Example or Connection: _____

_____

_____

Word: _____ | My Understanding 1 2 3 4

Definition: _____

Example or Connection: _____

_____

_____